Love From Every Angle

By
Wendy L. Wotring

Copyright © 2008 by Wendy L. Wotring

Love From Every Angle
by Wendy L. Wotring

Printed in the United States of America

ISBN 978-1-60647-725-0

All rights reserved solely by the author. The author guarantees all contents are original and do not infringe upon the legal rights of any other person or work. No part of this book may be reproduced in any form without the permission of the author. The views expressed in this book are not necessarily those of the publisher.

Unless otherwise indicated, Bible quotations are taken from The New International Version of the Bible. Copyright © 1984 by Holman Bible Publishers.

www.xulonpress.com

DEDICATION

To my children, Kristen Lyn, Derek Haddon
and Britt Ashlyn

Thank you for your lives of inspiration
and your heartfelt love.

ACKNOWLEDGEMENT

I am very thankful God gave me my husband, Mark, who leads our home with love and God's principles. He has been so patient with me during the writing of this book. He encourages me, prays for me and supports all my endeavors.

Britt Ashlyn has helped me with editing and has taught me so much about working with a true professional.

I would be remiss if I did not acknowledge my parents, Ben and Marie, and my mother-in-law, Ruth. Their lives shine. They have taught me so much. What a privilege to be their child.

Ann, Pam, Susan and Brenda, thank you for your help and encouragement.

TABLE OF CONTENTS

Introduction xi
"Put Me In, Coach" 15
Common but Powerful 19
The Dump 25
Picture in Mind 29
A Beautiful Outcome 33
In the Name of Duty and Care 37
Lighten Up 43
Opportunities Taken 47
God's Steps to Waiting 51
Ready for Spring 57
The Events of Our Lives 61
The Peter Pan Syndrome 65
At Home with Him 71
Love for Eternity 75
Satisfaction 79
The Potters Pig 83
The Gift of God's Forgiveness 87
"I Love You This Much!" 93
Mismatched 99
Created Individuals 103

The Sisters..107
Under Watchful Eye....................................113
It's Only a Scratch......................................117
The Treasure Box.......................................121
Shape and Form 127
The Little Things..131
Show Me What to Do 137
Beauty is Fleeting 143
The Favorite Blouse...................................147
Come Clean..151
Anchored in Love 155
Savior Alone...159
A Dog's Day Out..165
Tall Candles 169
Smoothing Rough Edges............................175
Tender Heart...181
Final Thoughts 189

INTRODUCTION

When I began writing this book, I decided there were a few things that are important for all of us to know. First, God is not like us. He is indeed the *Holy Other*. He is righteous and just in nature. His holiness distinguishes His separateness from us into a whole other category we do not fully understand. He is far above us in thought and action. His righteousness declares that He is incapable of wrongdoing. He is ethically perfect and morally pure. He does not defer to a higher cause or being because He is the ultimate source. Embodied in His remarkable Spirit, God has perfect knowledge and all power. He is present in all places at all times. He has creative abilities beyond our thought and love too deep and wide for us to measure.

    Second, He is just in all His engagements with us. Unlike the school yard bully or disingenuous friend who will continually point the finger to remind us of our lowly flawed character, God is gentle with our weaknesses. Humans expect a judge and jury to sentence the guilty, yet He knows our sins and

Love From Every Angle

---

grants forgiveness for all those who are repentant. In Hebrews 8:12 He tells us, "For I will forgive their wickedness and remember their sins no more." He also says in Psalms 103:12 that He will remove our sin "as far as the east is from the west, so far has He removed our transgressions from us." When outsiders or our hearts condemn us, we know there is one who has already paid the penalty for our transgressions. *He* is witness, judge and jury.

I have often wondered at the power of God's love that compelled Him to send His Son Jesus from the glories of the heavenly realm to become one of us to shed His blood to cover the sins of all who have sought Him throughout the ages. The perfect environment was His, and yet He was willing to do this to redeem us and bring us back into fellowship with Him.

Those who seek His presence and accept His sacrifice enjoy a relationship that goes beyond the boundaries of anything we can encounter here on earth. It is lasting, fruitful, encouraging and enjoyable. This amazing love, beyond our human nature, is what makes the very essence of His being something to admire, pursue and desire.

Have you longed for someone who would love you unconditionally and allow nothing to separate you from this love? Let me tell you that the God of heaven and earth, the one who gave you breath and life, is knocking at the door for you. Let Him in. He wants to commune with you and love you beyond all comprehension. Some of you know what I am talking about and have already discovered this amazing love. Isn't it wonderful?

> *"Oh God, how is it that you are so merciful to us who violate your laws every day?*
> *Truly you are the one to be worshipped and adored."*

It has been a treat for me to record the encounters in this book and share them with you. I have thought of each of you and want you to know about the excitement in God we can experience. As God shows Himself to us and through us, we step out of ourselves and into Christ. We become the student and God our teacher. The all-knowing Father will be our guide.

I chose the title of <u>Love from Every Angle</u> because I am intrigued at every turn in my life by the many facets of God's love and the masterful way He presents Himself to us. It is love that surpasses our imagination and holds our attention that enables Him to pierce through our world to bring us into His. Perhaps there is a wonder within you that has you questioning why the name of Jesus brings controversy and yet remains tried and true, always interesting and eternal. Millions have experienced Him and found that there is never any angle they can anticipate in which He will reveal love to us. These different ways of revelation He uses in our lives creates a longing to seek Him and keep Him fresh every day.

Many of the sketches in this book are personal stories and all the scriptures are true. Jesus is real and new every morning. To wake up and start a day is to enjoy Him, to learn something different about His character and walk in confidence knowing-He is the one leading, loving and calling me home to Him for always. Like the prodigal son's father, God waits and watches out and over the fields for us to return. We just have to realize that where He is there is security, satisfaction and sonship.

For some of us, it takes a while to decide whether or not Jesus is a true reality. Better to discover that here and now rather than later when we have no more choices. God does not promise that we will never encounter danger, physical illness, heartache or pain. Instead, He promises to be our friend and strength throughout every event. He promises to make a permanent change in us and show us the great way to view life and how to live wisely.

I hope this book is a blessing to you and that you can relate to some of the things I have brought out. Above all, that you will believe God's promises. It is harder than ever to see this rich country we live in and think we have a need beyond what we can do for ourselves. For many there isn't much we cannot get at a store to fill our wants and desires. For all there is emptiness within the heart that only Christ can fill.

I pray that Jesus will fill in the blanks and answer the questions you may have for Him. He is a prayer away.

In His Grace,
Wendy L. Wotring

"PUT ME IN, COACH!"

What a great job! How many of us love to hear those words! You've worked so hard and you know what? It shows! I think of the many people that influence a person's attitude in life and the most memorable remarks we enjoy are those of appreciation. Perhaps there was a special teacher who saw leadership qualities in you, and praised your efforts as they nurtured you along, or a neighborhood garden club member who loves coming to your house to glean from the fruits of your labor. It's a great feeling.

Although I am not a sports enthusiast I do love to go to the games and spend time with my friends who are. I am truly humbled when I listen to them spouting off a player's record of wins, with whom he has played, what his injuries have been, his ranking in the standings, his relationship with other players and the coach, who has traded him and what his strengths are. I want to give my friends a hand so to speak. It's quite impressive. Although I am in the dark at times I listen and try to grasp some sense of the player's worth in the sport's world. At the end of the evening, I have had a good time and been among the knowledgeable.

It's very interesting to me as I watch the fans. They run the full gamut from young families with tiny kids to high school students out on a date and the very serious minded involved fans who have traveled far to see their favorite team score the "big" one. While at the game, I wish I had taken the time to follow these players and know their stats, but that feeling soon fades and all I really care about is with whom I am enjoying my evening. They are my stars, my family and friends.

If you take notice, the players are pumped and ready to show off their hard work and get in the game. There is always someone leaning over the coach's shoulder and hoping to be sent out where he can score for his team and perhaps make history; hence the phrase "Put me in, Coach!"

It's really a lesson in life, isn't it? The coach has worked with these players day and night to build up their confidence with work-out sessions and pep talks. Their coach, who is also their mentor, knows his players strengths and forms the team's line-up accordingly. He wants them to come to practice on time and work the full hours. He expects their very best effort so that on the day that truly counts, they are prepared to go out and win. He wants nothing to disrupt their concentration during the long period of training. They are to get the proper rest, eat right and reach their goals. A coach is there to make sure that he instills the importance of the team concept and thereby strengthen them as a unit. He continues to work with each player as an individual specifically working with their particular needs.

It's a shame to watch some players abuse the privilege of belonging to sports clubs and never take the responsibility for their rebellious actions that are detrimental to their fellow athletes and disappointed fans. On the other hand, it is heart warming to hear one give a thankful interview after the game crediting the effort of coach, fellow players, hard work and fans. Listening to such a humble person gives the game a good name and sets a great example for our children watching.

I am reminded of my coach in high school. He was a proponent of hard work and consistency. I was in boarding school at the time so I observed him in all situations. He had the uncanny ability to see potential in every student yet so subtle in his efforts you were blindsided into involvement. He truly led a life that was worthy of your effort to please him. If he was interested in having you try something he knew you would say you were incapable of doing, he would ask you to come along and help him with a project he might like to try on the student body. He made you feel special and important without stroking your ego. Before you realized what he had done, you were the one on the sidelines whispering in his ear "Put me in, Coach."

God, in a very similar way, works quietly and deliberately to bring along the desire to follow Him. Perhaps we don't notice Him at first, nor do we care to get involved, but He never gives up hope on us. He

Love From Every Angle

uses His subtle ways to bring us along with training wheels if need be until we are stronger and able to understand what this relationship with Him is all about. His tactics are the best and His game plan for life's road is unbeatable. God sent His best, His son. Don't try to outsmart Him for His ways are not ours. Isaiah 55:8 and 9 says "For my thoughts are not your thoughts, neither are your ways my ways, declares the Lord. As the heavens are higher than the earth, so are my ways higher than your ways and my thoughts than your thoughts."

Be alert as He puts you through the paces and take His direction with pride. When the day comes for you to recall all that training and put it into practice, your heart will be ready to serve because the efforts on the field paid off. As you stay close to the eternal coach now, perhaps you will be the one anxious to do His bidding out of love for the one who stood by your side through thick and thin. An excited energy will fill you as you ask Him to put you in the game.

COMMON BUT POWERFUL

There are certain people that leave us with a warm memory of an eventful life. I can get so engrossed in listening to the telling that it stays with me for a long time. An uncle might tell of his adventures as a boy in the wild open land of the far north. Another might expound on the time he was one of the passengers on a near fatal plane accident and lived to tell about it. Remaining nervous about flying for so many years his palms would sweat and he would turn ashen with fear at the thought of entering the airport. Oh how the story builds and draws you in as if you were right there and it was you going through the adventure or tragedy. If the story teller is gifted a room can take on a stillness as quiet listeners gather around. There is nothing like it.

Have you ever heard someone say he wished he could be a fly on the wall to witness something from which he had been excluded? Great events of history would have come to life if we could have witnessed them unnoticed like that fly on the wall. Recently National Geographic telecast the unearthing of King Tut's tomb. Archeologists raised his mummified body from the tomb and used modern forensic science and artists to reconstruct the face of the boy king at his time of death. Actors were used to portray life so many years ago in Egypt. Sitting with my husband and friends as we watched the television program made me think I would like to have been that fly on the wall. Life was so different, it drew me in. How interesting it was to see how our modern scientists put the puzzle pieces together to reach their conclusion of how this boy king died so young. It took a team of men and women to fit its mystery together. There were many possibilities and each had to be explored.

This brings me to my point for you today. I have a dear friend with a picturesque testimony. It is a common one, but perhaps not many of us would think so. We are often more interested to hear famous heroes tell of foxhole conversions or football stars leaving fame and fortune to serve God and Him alone. We listen with intensity and think if someone so famous, so beautiful, talented or wealthy could come to the realization that there is more out there than the life they are living then perhaps it is good enough for me. I've often wondered why we need such sensationalism to stimulate the mind and heart. The bigger the story, the larger impact it seems to have on humanity.

Benton thought he had it all. He had a lovely wife, daughter and beautiful home. He was successful in business and generally speaking an all around pretty great man. Law abiding, Benton was clean in his dealings, and a good friend. God was good, but not necessary for him. His wife had found God to be tangible, real and alive. Good for her he imagined, but what does that have to do with me? Let her have her thing and I will enjoy the benefits of the change God has made in her life. Why not? At times he would read Bible tracts his wife had around the house and they might discuss something she had found to be true, but still Benton did not realize his need for the God of the Bible. There were several popular books circulating at this time. One book told the story of a Gang leader in New York City whose whole life changed because he came to understand God loved him. <u>The Cross and the Switchblade</u> was a good read but Benton thought "I am not a gangster. This does not apply to me. I do not need to be rescued from a life of crime. We are worlds apart." Brenda, his wife, prayed.

How <u>The Late Great Planet Earth</u> by Hal Lindsey got into their home, neither Benton nor his wife, remember. Benton picked it up and began to read. A fascination with the "End Times" was his. Hal Lindsey made reference to Scripture several places in his book. One Scripture that caught Benton's attention was Mathew chapter 25 where Jesus talked about the separation of sheep and goats. Benton went to a Bible. He read about it in his room upstairs, alone. Although this is a reference to nations, Benton understood the concept of being turned away by God. He would hear that still small voice as God spoke to his heart. "You are as much a goat as this Nicky Cruz; gang leader was that you read about in <u>The Cross and the Switchblade</u>. Alone in the room, Benton agreed with God and determined he didn't want to be outside of God's fold. An historical happening was taking place that day in the books of God's recording. An open heart by God's appointment was set free and Benton understood what God meant for him. The thought that God would make him do what he did not want to do, vanished from his mind that day. He told the Lord "I don't want to be a goat. I want to be one of your sheep and follow you no matter where you lead me."

No one's repentant story is quite the same. Our encounters with the Savior are all our own. God uses what will be effective in our particular situation. Some stories are broadcast. Some are never heard of, but all are a great and mighty work of God leading us to our glorious salvation conclusion. Through this book about "End Times" that stirred his heart with provoking thought and Bible references, his wife's loving prayers and patience to let God do His work in her husband, Benton was brought along in his journey. He became like a flower opening in the light of Christ. He was no longer averse to God becoming his life's love. The boasting he felt in his accomplishments and possessions he treasured didn't have the same importance they once held. He could say with Paul in Galatians 6:14 "May I never boast except in the cross of our Lord Jesus Christ, through which the world has been crucified unto me, and I to the world." He knew now whether he was a gangster, business man, rich or poor he needed Jesus Christ as his Lord.

More powerful than the unearthing of an ancient king's tomb, our lives are raised from the dead as God breathes everlasting life into the souls of men who are willing to surrender to God and bow the knee. Benton was able to experience with joy the change that had taken place as explained in II Corinthians 5:17 "Therefore if anyone is in Christ, he is a new creation; the old has gone, the new has come!"

For King Tutankhamen it took a team of experts in their field to recreate the face of the boy king in his last hours piece by piece and much time to figure out the mystery of his demise. For Benton, the piecing together of each event which led to his enlightened heart, it took the Father, Son and Holy Spirit, a team of <u>One</u>.

THE DUMP

On a Saturday morning you can usually find my husband and me at Lowe's or Home Depot, but most assuredly and more often than I care to say, visiting our home away from home, the Wake County Dump. You see, we are creating, building, repairing and perhaps dreaming in our present home. If you do these things it will include journeys to the wastelands. Many times with leather gloves we are hauling sheetrock, boards, old flooring, doors, etc…down our steps and unto the trailer at the top of our driveway. Once loaded down, we tie down our precious throwaways and away we go. There is a usual stop at the fast food drive thru for a drink. We continue talking about how much farther along we are with our project, how much we have on our backs, with the prospect of losing that burden soon. It's actually a happy fluttering feeling. Down Durant Road we go and into the waste facility. Once we go through the gates we are in another world. There are different directions for different items that we are to drop off, but the one we take most often is straight

Love From Every Angle

---

up the mountain of trash and junk. We know that there we will have sweet release. When we arrive at the top, we are there with our friends, the White Sea Gulls, as beautiful as ever. We unload our trailer and usually flop back in the truck remarking about our lovely birds. How do they stay so white and clean living among the mounds of trash?

One particular day, I was most intrigued with the blue sky and the thousands of white birds against the green hills with houses carefully tucked in among the trees. The horizon and above was where the beauty lay. I could not help but put all these sights together and be reminded of the study I was working on this year in the Old Testament. I would never have noticed it if my eyes had been down cast. Seeing just the junk and focusing on *it,* would have kept my mind there. However, I saw the horizon and the beauty and hope above. The birds kept their distance until they saw something they wanted. They were flying purposefully above the mounds of junk and trash on the ground.

In this life we are in the process of being made new. We must constantly get rid of the old as we take on the new. We must not think of this as nasty or distasteful. There is beauty even in this.

Moses had an encounter on the mountain when God spoke to him out of the burning bush. He told Moses to remove his sandals because he was standing on Holy Ground. Abraham and Isaac went to the mountain top to meet God where He established His faithfulness and holiness. God revealed His holiness again at Mt. Sinai with the children of Israel as He gave them His law.

You too, can have a picture to remind you of God's holiness. God works His process of sanctification to make us holy. He is getting rid of the old as He makes room for the new you. Remember I told you my husband and I are creating, building, repairing and dreaming in our home? God is doing the same in us. As we look upward to the Father, we will see the beauty in the process.

Remember the birds? There were so many. It was interesting that here they were, living and rooting around among all that garbage and trash, but to the ordinary eye, they looked clean almost as though they were living in an uncontaminated science lab. We can be fooled by appearances. Underneath the fluff of silken feathers there is dirt in their claws and underbelly. In order for the Christian believer to receive God's protection from our surroundings, we must respond to the gift of God's grace and wear the clothes of righteousness He provides for us. If we are not careful to listen and obey Him we can become sullied by the world. We may look clean like the birds, but our heart can be far from Him. We don't want to be like the birds that merely look clean. We want to ask God to do the work in us that makes an old and sinful being new and right before Him. When we cooperate with God the power of His holiness enables us to get rid of the junk in our lives making room to be filled with more of Him. We are constantly around a wicked and sinful world, but He has the power to keep us *white* even then.

I know that we are not the Patriarchs, but they are there to give us an example of God's power and holiness. When they yielded their lives to Him, they were able to do great and mighty things for their God. They chose to be His vessels here on earth. There is no reason why you and I can't see God's work in our lives no matter where we are, in a dump, in the grocery store, in our work environment or at home. We can sense our need to get rid of the junk in our lives as we encounter Him during any 24 hour period.

There are some bright days and some dark overcast days when we go to the landfill. It doesn't make any difference what the day is like. The landfill is still there and we continue to do the work. His work in us continues all the time, in the dark times and in the sunny times. He is continually cleaning out and moving in.

Philippians 1:6 says "Being confident of this, that he who began a good work in you will carry it on to completion until the day of Christ Jesus."

PICTURE IN MIND

Every day I look into the picture above the fireplace mantle in our family room. I purchased it many years ago in an antique store not too far from my home. I liked the colors and that it was a signed watercolor with the original glass, but mostly for the serene feeling it gave me. The scene is one at dusk on a secluded lake. I have tried to figure out whether or not its location is in the north or south. I don't know which it is, but I know it triggers my memory of days with my brother, Albin. My husband, our children and I would travel to Maine every few years, usually in early August, to visit my mother and father and also my brother and his family. While there, we often made a trip over to my brother's lake house for a picnic. We enjoyed the private little spot at the end of the wooded trail with the panoramic view of the lake. Al was always excited to show us something new he had discovered since we were there last. We often dreamed of moving there to be closer to family and perhaps working together. Once in a while Albin would take out his canoe and we would paddle out on the lake. The view, being so beautiful, engendered stillness within us. The water was refreshing and the ripples in the water seemed to go on and on.

Now my picture looks so much like the area we visited, that gazing into it, I am almost there with an expectation of a canoe coming around the corner at any moment. The glow of the moon reflected on the glassy water brings thoughts of a quieter life and another time we thought was quite free of the hurried life of city living. Maine can do that for you. These visits are filled with sweet memories of family, fun and lots of laughter. Al has always been a great story teller. He and my husband would swap tales of the outdoor life they both enjoyed. Back home and the vacation over, we were soon into the regular work week and our children's activities. That was our life and we loved it.

I have placed that picture in a spot in my home where I can study it several times a day. It helps to remind me that we need time to reflect and be at peace in our lives. God wants us to take time to meditate on Him and be assured in our hearts of the sacrifice He made for our well being. Sin can keep us on a treadmill going nowhere with nothing of lasting value to Him. We would do best to get off and take a trip to the cross, drop the heavy load we carry and think on the wonderful things He has done on our behalf. Memories and meditation on His deeds and His Word will put you in a frame of mind that brings peace and comfort to the inner self. The passages in Psalm 119 encourage us to do that very thing with regularity. David knew the importance of spending time with God. One such verse you might be interested in asking God to do for you is Psalm 119:18 which asks of the Lord to "Open my eyes that I may see wonderful things in your law." If you ask this of Him and search the Scriptures with the intent of learning His ways, He will guide you. Don't be discouraged if you don't know much about God. He will be the one that will increase your knowledge and broaden your understanding. Your heart will be filled with love and assurance. You will reach the spot, if you will, at the end of the trail where we rest with Him in perfect serenity.

Take time to schedule regular visits with God either in the morning or evening. Meditate on the reflections of the water of life He so freely gives and you will be better able to meet your days work with a mindset free of cluttered care. If you have to travel far into a quiet place to get away from the hurried life, do it. This may mean getting up before the house is full of the noise brought about by the hustle and bustle of the day. You will be so glad you did. Taking time out of your schedule to meet with the Savior should not be an inconvenience. It will stretch you and help bring things into proper perspective. You'll have a memory stamped on your heart of more important things in this life. Take time to hear Him and let Him speak to you in the stillness. The benefits of the living water He supplies go on and on as the ripples on a lake. You'll have much to talk about, you and He. Spending time at the Lord's feet each day will bring you to a place you will grow to enjoy most of all. You will want to revisit that time with Him again and again. Each interlude with Him will show you something new and different. You will awaken to a new insight of Him and He will speak truth to your heart so that your day makes sense.

A BEAUTIFUL OUTCOME

Anxious to get my yard in shape, I have learned many things about weeds, rocks and onions. Let me begin by saying "They are everywhere!" Living in our home for several years, we are beginning to master the yard by finally planting a suitable grass that seems to have a strong constitution and manages to build a healthy root system while dormant in winter. This is great news! However, by this time of year I am preparing to begin the good fight that will again rid our lawn of these weeds and bare spots. It's not easy you see — we have a very steep yard and pine trees. Steep yards can be a challenge because of their inefficiency to hold moisture for very long and the sun hits our yard dead on. The pine trees make it difficult to grow grass beneath them because of their acidity. Those aren't the only problems. I believe the onions and weeds work together to the annoyance of us home owners. Where are they coming from? Hoe hum.

Out I go with my tools in hand and begin to dispose of and separate these bothersome items from the healthy grass that we've newly planted, more to still plant, and other already established grass. Toiling in the early mornings and at times in the evening it is not hard to think that they are teaming up against me for their rights. Perhaps, I imagine, at night while I am sleeping exhaustedly from the work the day before, they are stretching their limits as they struggle to survive. As I am concentrating on one section, they are quick to take hold of another portion of ground. They spring up and spread out in no time at all.

I have different tools to help me. First, is the rake I use to prepare the ground for its new plugs of grass. Second, I use my stainless steel hand tool to uproot any nasty weeds in the area I am working on. Next, is a plug hand tool. Together, my husband and I dig up a spot with this tool and plant healthy 4-inch grass squares. We work for several days moving along the ground in a pattern. Although tools are great for broad areas, it takes careful handling of the ground to dig out small rocks, pinecones and young clover. This calls for full fisted involvement. While continually sorting out these various things in one part of the lawn, they are thriving in another vulnerable area. If these items are not pulled out it leaves little hope for the baby roots of this super grass to take hold and hang on until they are secured in the rich dirt, watered daily and bathed in sunshine. Young grass doesn't need interference from ne'er-do-wells.

No matter how long I spend on my knees clearing the area of rocks and weeds there are still more of them to be removed. In fact, the more I am watching for them—the more I see. It is just this longing for a better lawn. I find myself looking, clearing and picking up anything that would bother the little seedlings. I would imagine that is how God protects and nourishes us. We are His garden and He tends to us. The seedlings in our lives are small awakenings to His will and plan for us. He does not get discouraged as we might become. He just goes about His work to weed out what is hindering our growth and separating the rocks and weeds from the spark of life He placed in our hearts from the moment we accepted His vision for us. This is how our sin is then exposed and His solutions solve the problem area. It is a regular daily exercise. Our job is to soak up the water of His Word and bathe in His sunshine and grow, grow, grow! When we say "yes" to Jesus we acknowledge His continual work in us. He helps clear up wrong thinking, and understand His ways. He uproots the nasty so the rich area of new growth strengthens and matures choking out the things that keep us from being spiritually healthy such as weeds in an unattended yard.

This is how God deals with His children. He wants to see us flourish in His light. He wants to rid our hearts, where He makes His home, of the things that would hinder our growing strength in Christ. He tends to our needs and watches with great care. He as the farmer, churns our earth just enough so that the unsightly is recognizable and can be dealt with. He wants our roots planted so they can go down deep into the rich nourishment He has provided for us.

Have you ever thought of yourself cared for in such a way by a loving God? It is He who knows what we need. It is His hands that hold us, His hands that feed us, and His hands that will supply. He is the one that pulls out the onions in our life and plants a new strong foundation in which we can blossom. From the beginning of our season in Him and as we grow, He will be making note of our progress and feeding us with that which He sees necessary. He desires for us to be exposed to His garden remedies. He wants to see to it that our lives have grown more fully and lovelier each year.

We cannot always see what is happening at ground level, but God knows and is weaving a pattern that forms the green growth of maturity. The overall truth is that as we yield our lives to God's care we will become like Him, as the gardener becomes one with the garden. Let's give thanks that His hands are at work in our lives and that He is pruning, weeding and fertilizing for a beautiful outcome. John 15:1 and 2 says, "I am the true vine, and my Father is the gardener. He cuts off every branch in me that bears no fruit, while every branch that does bear fruit he prunes so that it will be even more fruitful."

IN THE NAME OF DUTY AND CARE

Let me reminisce for a moment with a family story that has brought both humor and truth.

My brother and his family live in Maine and have for more than four decades. While I was still in high school, Albin, my brother, was there and living in his 200 year old house with his wife, Diana, and their four girls Deborah, Cynthia, Cheryl, and Jennifer. They had two dogs; one a German Shepherd, and the other a Doberman Pincer. Over the years they've had cats, different dogs and raised a few sheep. Our entire family has always liked animals and has had some sort of pet indoors or out. We have always treated our animals more like people, expecting them to understand the reason for doing what we do for them and talking to them as if they are our children. Of course we know they are not our children, but our love for them makes them just another member of the family. They seem to sense our genuine commitment to them.

Love From Every Angle

Al had a particular sheep that did not act with predictability. What a shock! He was temperamental and did not always cooperate with the plan you had for him. He could not be trusted to be a gentle soul, nor did he trust or understand your intentions. He was the ram and would protect the ewes.

At first, Albin's family kept the sheep on their property in an enclosed area, but eventually moved some of them to a larger area on our parent's property down the road. When my brother could not come down to replenish the sheep's water, my father would fill a large bucket and carry it to them. Now and then Dad was responsible for feeding the sheep on his property, but that job was usually done by my brother's family.

My parents first moved to Maine after my sister, Dale, had married, Brad. My husband and I had moved again with our family, this time to North Carolina. After moving to Maine they settled in and planted a large vegetable garden. Mother would can most of the produce they grew to use in the year ahead. Dad would till the black soil and work the ground making straight clean rows. He liked things to line up and be uniform as well as functional. Quite the perfectionist, when things did not go right, it frustrated him. He liked continuity.

Now in this story, I must tell you that my father loved the sheep and looked after them with gentle care. He would give one of them a tap on the top of the head now and then with the empty plastic bucket when retrieving it for a refill. He'd have a one sided conversation, grab the horns of the ram and would say "How ya doing Ole Bean?" in a playful way. Dad was affectionate and a very funny man. At times he would get them all riled up as if he were playing with a pack of puppies and they would run around and knock all the fence posts down. Although he thought of them all as a pet such as a dog with a ball or cat with a string, they could not understand the game. They did not respond well to his humor.

This particular day Dad filled and carried the water bucket to the sheep in his usual manner. The supply from the worker's hand was always reliable and timely, but the reaction to it was uncertain. The day was sunny and hot. Dad's tender heart knew they needed a fresh bucket of cool clean water. His intentions were pure and thoughtful, but a pattern had been formed with Dad's quick moves and "tap" of the bucket. With watchful eye, Bo, the ram saw him coming with that bucket in hand. Dad whistled a tune as he crossed the field signaling the sheep he was on the way with the much needed drink.

Oddly, according to Dad, Bo, lowered his head and charged him as my father came closer inside the fence. Flying upward and everywhere the spilled water went splashing all over Dad. The bucket slung out of his hands as Bo bolted into Dad's kneecap with great force. Down like a wounded soldier, the relief effort was dashed. Dad thought his knee was broken. It wasn't, but he was so put out with that ram! "What in the world was that all about? All I wanted to do was bring you water!" I know the ram's reaction was a shock to Dad, but Bo had his day in court. Perhaps he was responding to that bop on the head as if to say "Don't do that again!"

Things in life can make anyone cautious when hurt or there is a misunderstanding. Dad did not want to hurt the sheep, but was simply playful and unaware that his actions signaled an alarm to the ram of annoyance rather than fun.

When God sends someone to bring us a cool drink of water, have we reacted in anger or held God at bay because others have irritated us? Perhaps we cannot see the blessings of water to our thirsty soul. A hurtful past can cause us to see an empty bucket ready to land on our head and once again squelch our hopes. We are unable to see the potential within the Savior's arms.

Sheep have many fears. They are weak and defenseless. They will not drink from running water and are alarmed by so little a disturbance. They are dumb animals and easily go astray. I am sure these are some of the reasons God compares them with the human heart. He calls us sheep and like them we need to be told to "fear not" because God knows we often do.

Of course, we know that God is not in the habit of bopping us on the head in jest, but it is reasonable to think there are some things He must allow to get our attention. If we just knew that when God is near, we are safe. When He comes to us, as we draw nigh to Him, it is for our benefit. I believe we must pray for an understanding of reality when it comes to God's blessings for His children.

Boregarde was reacting out of instinct. Many times our instinct is to throw up a defense as well. We don't need to do that when it comes to our relationship with God. No matter how difficult our walk on earth is, God will be by our side supplying us with buckets full of tools of the faith, love, meaning and understanding. We have only to give Him a chance to put the bucket down. He'd like us to drink from the well of His resources.

When the apostle Paul was writing the early church in Ephesus he expressed a prayer for his fellow believers in Christ. "I keep asking that the God of our Lord Jesus Christ, the glorious Father, may give you the Spirit of wisdom and revelation, so that you may know him better. I pray also that the eyes of your heart may be enlightened in order that you may know the hope to which he has called you, the riches of his glorious inheritance in the saints, and his incomparably great power for us who believe." Ephesians 1:17,18 and 19a.

Bo would never get to that point. No matter how old and experienced he may be as a ram, he would never reach understanding as a human being. God gives us understanding and wisdom as we trust Him for His unlimited bounty.

LIGHTEN UP

One would think that reaching middle age meant a put together life. Our children are grown and grandchildren are abundant. Our house and garden should be getting to the "I'm satisfied" stage. The books we have wanted to read have been read and our recipe know-how is pretty set. But wait a minute, I'm describing Martha Stewart! Not so with most women. There is always something around the corner telling us that there is a better way of doing the things we have so long been trying to perfect. It seems we are on fast forward and brevity of time is having us run to catch up or stay up! The day has begun and before we realize it, it is dinner time. In the rapid pace of our day we sometimes say things we wish we could take back. "Woops, did I say that?" Now don't get defensive, it happens to us all. Keeping a sense of humor is important so that we don't get hurt or be hurtful to others. I have often thought that God has a keen sense of humor and built one right into us, for laughter is the best medicine. It has been said that it is actually good for us to laugh. Proverbs 17:22a reads "a cheerful heart is good medicine." Life is quick and at times far too serious for us not to laugh some things off and get a kick out of ourselves and friends. I have the dearest of friends. God has truly blessed me with many. There is one particular friend of mine that tickles me so. If I am down or discouraged I have only to pick up the phone and hear her voice and we are immediately laughing about life. I never feel foolish around her or down in the dumps. Our husbands get along extremely well and we laugh about how different they are in looks and occupation, but they are just like brothers as Pam and I are just like sisters. From the time we met at a swim meet our children were participating in about 23 years ago, somehow we clicked and we enjoy many of the same hilarious moments. Our children love this couple and I know the feeling is mutual. God makes us all different and puts various combinations of people together to enjoy each other and Him. What a relief to have friends to clown with and share life and love no matter what. We are lifetime friends and we would do anything for this couple and their family.

I am sure there are those who are of the opinion that Christians are solemn and stiff. They have their heads in the Bible so much they don't know what is going on with the present world. Do they think that Christians don't read the newspaper or keep up with current events? Each of us has hobbies and activities with family and the community we enjoy. We work hard and vacation just like anyone else. Perhaps some think people of faith are so intense, that they are uncomfortable around them. To the world at large,

Christians appear to have tunnel vision and cannot enjoy fun or pleasure. Not so! Some of the most dedicated believers I know enjoy life with laughter and great times. Loving God doesn't mean that you can't be a part of a joke or give a great party.

Have you ever realized that Jesus was a social individual? He loved the time He spent with all types of people in different situations and circumstances. He was quite aware of the social issues of His time and used them to teach others how to unconditionally love those who were different. At times He was the gracious host cooking fish on the ocean shore for His disciples early in the morning. Other times He welcomed men with questions such as Nicodemus, a Pharisee of the Jewish ruling council, Peter and Doubting Thomas. He gathered children to His side, expressing His love and open heart. Still many other times He was a man of compassion healing those who were sick and rejoicing with them. He joined the teachers of the law in the synagogue and debated deep subjects from the time He was only twelve. Jesus was a great listener and liked discussing a variety of subjects with others. The Gospel of John chapter 2:1-11 tells us that His first miracle was performed at the wedding of a friend. Now that is a happy occasion of which He took part! When confronted with the fact that this family was out of wine for their guests, Jesus kindly performed the miracle of turning the water into wine. This showed His glory and was thoughtful at the same time. He could have ignored their problem, but He chose to step up and be a friend in what could have been an embarrassing situation for the family of the groom. In those days the groom's family supplied the wine for the wedding festivities. All the people were amazed and thrilled as the party continued on. I am sure there was a show of astonishment as well as revelation of who Christ was for others. Verse 11 tells us that His disciples put their faith in Him.

Christians lead fulfilling lives and can be as engaging as the next person. They have reason to celebrate. There is joy in the moments and days lived for Christ Jesus. We do not need to be pumped up with fluff and glitter for there is a happy heart already. Proverbs 15:13a says "A happy heart makes the face cheerful."

So, my friend, enjoy each day with a happy heart attitude that expresses that you are getting more than you deserve. Appreciate the breath you are given and each moment of every hour. God has been generous with His mercy and blessings.

OPORTUNITIES TAKEN

While working on a project a week or two ago, I had a memory come to mind of a kindness shown to me. I hadn't even been looking for it, nevertheless it showed up in the front portion of that file we keep in our minds of times rescued. I remembered the words of a great old song which brought sensibility and hope to a sad heart.

Things are not always easily walked through especially when carrying a great burden. That is where I was. Feeling the weight of such distress, my bent spirit was having a difficult time. I had prayed and wept and felt a sorrow I had not known since my father-in-law had past away from a heart attack in 1975.

This memory helped me recall the wonderful encouraging words of Paul to the struggling churches of the New Testament. Paul was a motivator, full of zeal for the Lord Jesus. He wanted everyone to come to know the Savior for their own personal lives. When the young churches were off track and walking down the wrong road, he reminded them of the truth they believed in and helped them realize their position in Christ. With belief in the Savior as our conqueror, as well as guidance for life's situations we have hope like none other the world can give.

There are those times when we feel lost. Everyone does sometimes. It is then that we need a wakeup call. The reality we have in Christ feels distant. Thank God he doesn't want us to depend on our feelings because they have a tendency to change. He, on the other hand, does not change as it tells us in Hebrews 6: 17, 18 and 19a. He keeps His promises and is incapable of lying. "Because God wanted to make the unchanging nature of his purpose very clear to the heirs of what was promised, he confirmed it with an oath. God did this so that, by two unchangeable things in which it is impossible for God to lie, we who have fled to take hold of the hope offered to us may be greatly encouraged. We have this anchor for the soul, firm and secure."

Forgetting temporarily His faithfulness to His children I was in need of uplifting and someone knew that. As I lay on the bed I felt a hand touch mine. "I want you to listen" a voice said. I was handed a sheet of paper with a four line melody as my husband scooted across the covers and began to sing the words to an old chorus. This is what it says.

"Got any rivers you think are uncrossable?
Got any mountains you can't tunnel through?
God specializes in things thought impossible
And does the things that others cannot do."
Words and music by Oscar C. Elaiason

I sat up and took notice of the alarm ringing out. It was a transforming of my attitude as I was being reminded again that God is bolder, bigger and stronger than anything that enters our lives. He was once again the Faithful Lord.

I will never forget that four line song, nor the message it holds. Even the hymn writers knew the doctrinal truths of the words of the Bible as they penned songs that sang out such inspiration.

If one has ever been rescued from a fall it is not hard to remember the kind hand and strong footing that brought them to safety.

Are you an encourager? Is there someone that you could reach an arm out to in the storm of heartache or the pit? Sometimes all it takes is a song or an experience of your own tied to a Biblical fact that will change a person's perspective. If you have encountered difficulty and God has shown you His answers through prayer or His Word, it can be used for His glory and someone's benefit. God wants us to share our joy and peace with others so they too will see through the clouds to the sunshine of His face.

David's psalms are encouraging to read. They call out for God and name God's glorious attributes. They are a sweet testimony of God's grace and strength. Many years ago a friend shared with me the peace of heart that comes with reading 5 Psalms before laying my head to rest at night.

When we have opportunity, let's hold another's hand. May we speak clearly and softly of God's faithful and kind acts towards men of all sorts in all regions of the world. When we are in a position to do so, remind another of God's goodness and power to take on any task.

GOD'S STEPS TO WAITING

What is waiting on God all about? Wouldn't you agree it is a much over looked exercise in the Christian walk? Many times when all else seems to fail, we say "All we can do is wait..." We should say "What we should do is wait..." Yet, even though we know this to be true, we often place it aside as our last resort. I believe it is an important part of the core in the Christian faith walk. As far as I am concerned, waiting is an action word.

Our main source from which we gather strength for the journey is FEASTING. We must feast on the Word of God. We glean from God's wisdom and truth, encouragement, and light. He tells us in II Timothy 2:15 "Do your best to present yourself to God as one approved, a workman who does not need to be ashamed and who correctly handles the word of truth." When we do these things, we are able to piece together the riches God is talking about in His Word. What does the Word of God say, and what does He want to tell us. Feasting is the avenue we walk down in order to stand.

We cannot STAND on an empty stomach for long periods of time before we notice the hunger pangs that tell us we are in need of food. We stand by the bed of a loved one, we stand by the phone waiting for news, we need to stand for the truth of God's message that we have been digesting. However, we cannot stand on His Word if we do not know it and learn from it, neither can we do much standing if we do not first feed on God's Word to nourish our mind and heart.

God asks us to LISTEN. I have a grandson, Haddon, who went to Bible study with me when he was quite young. I would go to my class and he would go to his where he heard Bible stories that helped him learn about God and God's love. At the end of the day, before his parents, our son, Derek and our daughter-in-law, Amy, came to take him home, I had time to talk and play with Haddon. One particular day when he was with me, I wanted to reinforce the story he had learned that day in class. I brought out one of the books I had used with Derek when he was a child.

I began to ask Haddon questions about the kind shepherd reaching for the lost sheep. Haddon was playing with his toy dinosaurs. It appeared he was not paying attention to the story or picture I so loved. When I came to the question of how the sheep got stuck in the briars over the cliff, Haddon would say, "The man shot him." Finally after two tries, I told him to brush the toy dinosaurs aside and snuggle close to me and listen. He then immediately got the answer correct. It was not a matter of lack of intelligence; it was that he was distracted by the dinosaurs. Hebrews 12:3 tells us to "Consider him who endured such opposition from sinful men, so that we will not grow weary and lose heart." That means that by meditating on what we read in Scripture about Jesus, His reality is brought to our everyday lives. In fact, we are encouraged. God knows we are so easily distracted that He emphasizes our need to meditate on Him and His Word for our good.

PRAYER is the glue that holds each step together. My husband has done many renovations in our house of 25 years. The latest project has been the steps leading to the second floor. The original set was carpeted and poorly built. Mark removed the carpet from the steps and replaced the old steps with new red oak steps. As I watched him first measure twice and cut once, I noticed he not only nailed the steps down, but also glued. It reminded me of God's faithfulness in our waiting to stick tightly to us in order to see us through whatever circumstances we are experiencing. It also gives added strength to withstand life's pounding pressures as we lift requests and petitions up to Him.

God wants us to PRAISE Him in our waiting. He is good all the time. He is dependable, and follows through on His promises. His mercies endure forever. He is on His throne, ruling over the earth and heaven. He desires to be intimately involved in our lives. He is in control of all that goes on. When we praise Him our hearts are encouraged to know we serve a living, active God. He is then pleased with our love for Him.

Waiting on Him is faith in who He is and that what He says is true. We wait on Him in FAITH. Our faith is rooted in the sure truth of His Word. He wants us to show and give witness to His glory and power. This is perhaps one of the more difficult steps to take, yet so necessary. Faith is the backbone and bedrock of our relationship with Christ. Without it we accomplish nothing. Without faith we merely give lip service to an empty religious crutch. Hebrews 11:1 says "Now faith is being sure of what we hope for and certain of what we do not see."

We WORK for Him while we wait on our answers. We cannot sit idle in the hope that He will show us the way. Our work is faith in action. He constantly directs and guides as we go forward with our lives. Ephesians 4:12 tells us that God's people are to be prepared for service, so that the body of Christ can be built up. Also in Colossians 3:23 the Bible tells us "Whatever you do, work at it with all your heart, as working for the Lord, not for men." This does not mean that we don't go to work for a company or get involved with volunteer work. It simply means that whatever we do, we are to do it as though the Lord were watching and cares how we conduct ourselves. We are to do a good job at whatever God has us doing.

Finally there is REWARD in waiting. Isaiah 40:31 says "but those who hope in the Lord will renew their strength. They will soar on wings like eagles; they will run and not grow weary, they will walk and not faint." When I read that verse I want to whisper to the Lord "Teach me Lord to wait." I want to learn in my waiting by putting down the distracting things in my life that I am so tempted to focus on, and strengthen my spiritual muscles through walking God's way. His steps help me keep my eyes on Jesus. He will show me how to take things step by step as I follow His Word.

READY FOR SPRING

Some time ago, I strolled into one of my favorite stores in my neighborhood and looked around for something with that "spring feeling." I am sure you too have felt the doldrums of winter and have wanted a little pick me up. This was such a day. This is a store that does that for me every time I walk in. It has the latest in bright and cheerful things. It inspires me to think wonderful thoughts and gets my creative juices flowing. I don't always buy something, but I do browse a lot for ideas. A box of vivid pink rose petals caught my eye as I noticed some casually spread over a comforter on a white iron bed.

Winter's cheer is red and white and orange from bittersweet with green as a backdrop. Spring brings visions of white and pink, robin's egg blue, and yellow. I could see it all now with the trailing green ivy and moonflowers in a garden of color. I picked up the box and walked around. I love roses. They are stunning no matter where they are placed. I purchased the petals and walked out to my car. On my way home, I pulled the box out of the bag so I

Love From Every Angle

could look at each one. Little did I know how God would use my love for flowers and roses in particular to drive home a biblical truth to my mind and heart on Easter Sunday.

Sitting in the pew next to my husband I listened to our pastor describe a situation in Europe during the 17th century. Being a teacher of children and a lover of little nuggets I can tuck away, I leaned in with interest and learned something new. He was speaking of Christ and the very real fact that He did indeed die for our sake. Of course our pastor made sure that we understood Christ Jesus rose again and lives even now. He began to unfold the story of the Black Plague that swept across Europe. Not understanding the source of the plague nor germs and disease, doctors and loved ones were under the impression that the Black Plague was caused by contaminated air. Legend has it that the very ill patients were placed on a literal "bed of roses." The well gathered around them in a circle, holding hands. They moved hurriedly in one direction with the hope that this motion would stir up the fragrance of the roses and purify the air. They did not know that this devastating disease was caused by flea bitten rats. People of that day lived in filthy conditions, unaware of its threat to health. The story tells us that a man came up with a rhyme that describes the ritual they went through uselessly. It goes like this.

"Ring around the roses
Pocket full of posies
Ashes, Ashes, we all fall down."

Many during that horrific time died at the hands of the Black Plague. All the roses with their beauty and fragrance were not going to save them. I thought about my rose petals and the beauty they bring, of rituals and habits we live with, in our world. When someone is ill, we bring them flowers to cheer them up. We will all fall down one day. We may not be burned as the diseased bodies of 17th century Europe, but we will all return to ashes as the Word of God tells us in Ecclesiastes 3:20 "All go to the same place; all come from dust, and to dust all return."

Have we the right solution to save us? Hebrews 7:25 tells us "Therefore he is able to save completely those who come to God through him, because he always lives to intercede for them."

Some have written songs calling Jesus "The Rose of Sharon." I know that this flower is one of extreme beauty and fragrance. Roses in spring or any other time lift our spirits and bring life to any environment as well as put a smile on our face. Jesus does all of that and more. His sacrifice is life giving, His nature is love and His written Word is sweet to the senses. Won't you lay yourself at His feet and let Him lift you out of the doldrums? The stirring touch from this Rose brings eternal healing to the illnesses of man.

THE EVENTS OF
OUR LIVES

Sometimes, hearing of a great event in someone's life starts your day with a "Wow" factor. I pass them along when I hear them because it's encouraging and uplifting to everyone no matter what is going on in their own lives.

On a Saturday night in our recent past my husband and his dear friend, Randolph, decided to go to the car races. So off they went to South Boston, Virginia for a fun time of excitement. After talking with some of the drivers, a pit tour and cheering, the race was finished. They drove the hour and a half back home with nearly as much chatter and enthusiasm as they had during the main attraction.

Up the next morning my husband, Mark and I set out to go to church when Mark discovered he did not have his wallet and it was nowhere in the house. "We can't go anywhere until I take care of this" were his words as he first called Randolph to see if he had left it in the car. With no end to his search he sat down to begin the process of asking those in authority to put a hold on his credit cards. When he was finished doing that we drove to church. "Well there's nothing I can do except drive up there once more in hopes there is someone at the track on Sunday." That didn't seem likely, but Randolph insisted on driving Mark up to the track after church services.

On arriving, it appeared as though there was no one there, so they drove around the back and saw a woman by a trailer. While telling their sad tale, they asked her if she perhaps knew someone who could help them with their dilemma. Surprisingly, she told them she was the manager of the track and she was willing to unlock the gate. They searched the grounds where they thought they had been to no avail. They came to the stands to search the seats. Nothing was found, but there was still another place to look. After all, they didn't want to give this a brush off when they had come so far. While under the bleachers Mark looked up to point to where they had been sitting. Way above them, which seemed to be about 50 ft in the air, he saw his wallet resting on a steel beam between the seats and the ground. Somehow his wallet had fallen out of his jean pocket and landed securely on that narrow rod, a place that would have been difficult for anyone to find. Elated, he telephoned me relaying his good news. I then called Pam, Randolph's wife. We all were excited and didn't think it was by chance Mark noticed his wallet missing on a Sunday when the track is not open for business. That the woman was there and just happened to be the track manager was an added bonus! What a miracle and something to share with others. I have had many people express that it was just that.

Does God help us with of our concerns? Yes he does. Just having had a birthday, Mark had received this wallet from our Pennsylvania grandchildren, Lyndsey and Luke. On the front corner of this handsome wallet was a tiny silver emblem. This is what he saw glistening in the afternoon sun at the track on the narrow beam which supports the bleacher seats.

This reminded me of the section of Scripture found in Mathew chapter 6. It records Jesus speaking to the multitudes about worry. He knows our human nature is to fret. What would happen if someone were to get their hands on the credit cards, driver's license and other such pertinent information we need to run our daily lives? The right thing to do was pray and protect our assets until Mark gathered any further information. Rather than let the missing wallet upset him, they retraced their steps to see if they could locate the lost wallet. God had it resting right there on the beam.

I have returned to that section of Scripture in Mathew chapter 6 many times in my life. God clothes the lilies of the fields and feeds the birds of the air. He will take care to see us through each day no matter what concerns us.

Right in the middle of explaining the pitfalls of worry Jesus assures us of our incredible value to God. Mathew 6:26 says "Look at the birds of the air; they do not sow or reap or store away in barns, and yet your heavenly Father feeds them. Are you not much more valuable than they?"

Whether the wallet was found or not was up to God. We have only to give thanks for His mercy to us. God uses events, inanimate objects, people and His Word to effect the direction as well as purpose for our lives. Recognizing His hand in these matters is to picture the sudden appearance of a light bulb pop-up above our heads expressing an "I've got it!" The glow in our hearts comes from understanding that the caring Savior works in mysterious ways to shows us His presence. He lets us know that we have moved His Word from our heads to our hearts.

> Psalm 121:1 and 2 "I lift up my eyes to the hills-where does my help come from? My help comes from the Lord, the Maker of heaven and earth.
>
> Psalm 121:8 "The Lord will watch over your coming and going both now and forevermore."

Do you think that your problems or issues are of no concern to Him? Have you tried to do everything yourself? Do you have things that you habitually worry about? These are the very times that you need to go to Him and share all your concerns and cares. Nothing is too small or too big for Him. What a change in your outlook when you no longer have to worry about things beyond your control. Your help does come from Him.

THE PETER PAN SYNDROME

When I was a school girl, I enjoyed being in the choir and the traveling trio, leading the band, acting in plays and taking art class. Having an imaginative mind from birth, I was interested in all the fantasy acted out in the various roles I played. I played the role of Sleeping Beauty, a page, Maria in Sound of Music, acted in skits and my favorite, played the part of Peter Pan in Elementary School. These things were a lot of fun and hold great memories for me still. My husband and I continue to enjoy musicals, plays and the ballet.

Tinker Bell was a fascinating character wasn't she? We all would like to think that we could not only fly, but with a sprinkle of *pixie dust* bring happy thoughts to life. What power! Tiny as she was, it was not until she and her magic entered the picture that her fellow characters were able to fly and realize their dreams. Wouldn't that be a convenience we would all like to enjoy? With a sprinkle, the wave of a magic wand and happy thoughts, problems would be solved and escape into an imaginary world would be ours.

Today there has been an amazing shift in our culture and many have written books on the power positive thinking holds for all who are rearing children, battling illness and struggling in the business world. Visualize what you dream. What my mind can conceive, my body can achieve! Powerful preachers and speakers hold seminars couched in the name of the Lord giving uplifting presentations to forward thinkers with the hope of making their lives better with a few life savvy skills. "If you see your schedule is too full, just say "No" to people and give yourself the much needed break." I heard a famous preacher spout to thousands of faithful head agreeing fans. "You must take care of you. You deserve it!" As I listened to his motivational talk I got the impression that he was emphasizing the importance of looking out for Number One above all else. Taking care of one's self somehow gave the illusion of any problems we are weighed down with disappearing. There seemed to be a picture here of one's burdens, problems and just plain sin in open hands with palms up as if they were pixie dust and our breath, the wind that gives them flight into the atmosphere as they dissipate into the air. We would be wise to use common sense and business skills of proven value to better our tactics in handling organization and function, yet there is a vast misunderstanding when it comes to grasping what distinguishes a carnal man from a spiritually driven one. Although God wants each of us to be a whole being who functions smoothly, He is far more concerned that we possess a healthy spiritual heart. Many of these seminars deal with outward appearances that may catapult us into powerful positions if worked on, but God looks on the heart. Because man is who he is wherever he goes, businesses cannot change a person's inner being with just guidelines and motivational skill training. That is why many attend these meetings and come away unchanged. The outward man appears polished but the inward man, who we are, remains the same unless there is a God transformation.

Is this God, whose name is often lifted up during crisis and monkey see monkey do antics a mere good friend we pull from a hat who can be called on for favors with smiling faces and laughing giddiness? No, not at all! I feel so sorry when I see seemingly intelligent people staring into the face of leaders in the faith community expounding on and on with fluff and empty chatter as if that would be God's message to mankind. I want to say "Wake up from your fantasy oh silly audience! On the count of three I will say "reality" and you will come to your senses!" Peter Pan is merely a cute story for babes! Our problems don't fly away in the wind. We must settle into the cushion of God's assurance.

Although our culture here in America and the world changes and we must update our forces and plans, there has always been one book that remains timeless. Its content is always up to date in any era. It is the Word of God. Romans 15:4 tells us "For everything that was written in the past was written to teach us, so that through endurance and encouragement of the Scriptures we might have hope." God does not change and we are continually in need of the Savior to rescue us from our desperately sin-filled heart, not a new fashion line or palm held personal computer. His love remains forever, His promises are true forever and His ways work for any situation. I don't care whether you are in the corporate structure, an entrepreneur, organizational wizard, student, child or parent, His laws and unyielding pursuit of us continues throughout the ages. We are not going to sing our way into heaven, talk our way into heaven or fly to the skies and hope Saint Peter will have mercy on us at Heaven's gate. He will not let us in because we had a bad rap or manipulated our way through life. In fact it is not up to him at all. This notion is as empty as a fairy tale is to a grown-up. Good people cannot lean on their flawless record of good deeds or random acts of kindness. There truly is no amount of good intentions that will please God beyond total submission to Him. Isaiah 64:6 says "All of us have become like one who is unclean, and all our righteous acts are like filthy rags; we all shrivel up like a leaf, and like the wind our sins sweep us away." Now that is a twist isn't it? It is not that we can blow our sins away, but they sweep us away.

Here's the Good News. We have a God who can take care of that. He died for us and bore our sins in our stead. We look to Him and admit we are in need. Being sorry for the sinful state we are in, we can willingly turn to Him in trust for help and guidance wherever we are. We are made clean and become His forgiven children.

I hope you will consider these verses and ask Him to be your personal Savior. You can know and have complete assurance that Christ is the one you can trust in everyday.

I John 5:20 says "We know also that the Son of God has come and has given us understanding, so that we may know him who is true. And we are in him who is true- even in his Son Jesus Christ. He is the true God and eternal life."

Ask Him to take that active role in your life. You will be so happy you did. Find others that want to learn from God's Word and use it to guide their lives in a sinful world. Work and learn together. The experience will give you strength to live the reality of your new life in Christ.

AT HOME WITH HIM

I spoke with my mother yesterday. She seemed very positive. As we chatted, the subject of my father's condition came up. I asked her how he was doing physically and mentally. You see my father, Ben, suffers from Alzheimer's disease. They live together in a retirement home in Raleigh, N.C. They have been here since we moved them four years ago from their own farm house in Maine. As it was a large home and harder to maintain than they wanted to cope with, the decision to move closer to my husband, myself and our children was made. They have managed quite well where there are friends their age, prepared meals and numerous activities.

My mother is quite sharp at age 91 and for the most part she has been able to help my father reach his potential and live happily in their apartment. It goes without saying that there are many challenges that go along with this progressive disease. He tends to be confused and does not know where he is and forgets who my mother is periodically. Simple commands are difficult to understand for him now.

At times he has a great concern that his Connecticut State Police badge is with me and safe. These fretful thoughts are disturbing to my mother as it is hard for her to accept that this vital, vigorous, guitar playing man has changed into one so different. She cries, and many times it is helpful for me to be a loving daughter and visit simply to talk with her about the situation. There is a tendency for my mother to want to isolate herself. But my parents, so in love, remain by each other's side and cope together.

I have watched them deal with the struggles of disease and old age with admiration. My father was 92 in February. There are not many children so fortunate to have the example of parents who trust the Lord with their lives and take everything to Him.

I hold a memory close to my heart of my parents kneeling by their bed in prayer both in the morning and before slipping into bed at night. As a child, I would lie in bed or walk by their room and hear their prayers. I was comforted to know that the God my parents taught about was real to them and that they practice what they have tried to instill in me. Why would I want a life with Jesus Christ? I saw it worked out every day. Not only did they pray, but they were servants of the God they loved.

My mother was the first believer in her family. Begged to attend church and Sunday school by my sister, Dale, she went one Sunday to a nearby church and heard the truth of the Bible. Mom was moved by the compelling message of God's love and salvation. She continued to go back each week until she understood its reality. My father watched her life for a while and was soon convinced to give the Bible a chance. At age 7, I witnessed my parent's baptism and today still hear the words to the hymn sung "Trust and Obey, for there's no other way to be happy in Jesus but to trust and obey." It was not just a song, but a battle cry to serve the Lord God with all their hearts. I am so grateful that they decided to do just that and be an example to all who come around them.

I checked in with my mom about my father's condition. She said, "He woke me up several times last night. He kept coming over to me with his hand on mine to say, "Now by morning, we will be dead, but the Savior will take us home to be with Him." She and I laughed for a second in the kitchen at the simplicity of his matter-of-fact statement, yet there was a reassurance in it. Had we not known that somewhere inside that shell was the man, Benjamin Anson Davis, who trusted his life to the Lord Jesus Christ so many years ago, we might think that was just a night-long annoyance. Yet, it was a testimony of what the Spirit of God had sealed in his heart. "I love you, Ben. Let me be your guide, your Savior, friend and comfort."

We never know what may befall us. Difficult times will come our way. I am so thankful that God is able to handle the easy, the difficult, the tearful and the laughing events of our lives. My mother, Marie, and I have decided that his statement to her all night long was for a purpose. It gave Mom reassurance of Dad's mindset. At least he had his mind on things above, and Mom was glad for it. Colossians 3:1-3 says just what we knew had happened in Dad's life.

"Since, then, you have been raised with Christ, set your hearts on things above, where Christ is seated at the right hand of God. Set your minds on things above, not on earthly things. For you died, and your life is now hidden with Christ in God. When Christ, who is your life, appears, then you also will appear with him in Glory." I have heard that somehow, when a mind fails from disease, that the person can still remember Jesus when He has been their mainstay.

When Jesus left this earth thousands of years ago, He gave us a counselor, the Holy Spirit to comfort and guide. Hebrews 13: 5b tells us that God said, "I will never leave you nor forsake you." In John 14: 26 it says, "But the counselor, the Holy Spirit, whom the Father will send in my name, will teach you all things and remind you of everything I have said to you." Because Dad has followed Jesus, the truths he has studied are still with him. He knows them to be real. Thank you, Lord.

Post Script:
When I wrote this devotion, little did I know that 11 months later, Ben, then in a nursing home, would quietly slip into his Eternal home without fanfare. This precious Christian man who led his family by love's example was the father I am so proud to call my own.

LOVE FOR ETERNITY

I was raised in the beautiful state of Connecticut. I assumed that every little girl woke to crisp air and chilly mornings and everyone enjoyed the space between homes that I took for granted. Our town required each house to have at least two acres of land. The street signs could be just so large and the whole feel of the place was to remain quaint. We valued its charm and nothing or no one was going to widen roads or bring in a "commercial" atmosphere to spoil our artsy little community. There was an understanding between residents that we had a special place to live and it was up to us to keep it so. Many famous people have lived there and still do. They are close enough to New York City, but do not have to live in cramped quarters. Privacy is still an issue for the home owners, and there are numerous trees and long hidden driveways. One might never know they are living next to someone books are written about.

  Winters in this area are spectacular and the brilliant white snow stays for long periods untouched by plows or footprints excluding the main streets and shoveled driveways. The fall is just as wonderful with the most vivid colors you can imagine filling the trees. The yellows are golden and the reds are deep and purples rich. Each house has uniqueness and historical background. Never did I enjoy these things more than the freedom I had to ride with my friends on their horses. My family did not own a horse, but I loved to ride every chance I could. Most weekends were taken up with talking about horses, trying to persuade someone to just let me groom their horse or riding through the woods bareback with my friend and her pony. We were small girls riding double and singing to him as we rode all afternoon. Many times we would ride five miles into town through the woods and back again. Those days are so memorable. I dreamed about the next time I would have a chance to ride again and the hope of doing so kept me gleeful.

One of the things that we would talk about while riding was the vastness of the sky. We would take off on her pony and try to reach the point we thought was the other side of the sky covering. What seemed like a short distance never came closer. So strange we thought. We looked up at blue sky and billowy clouds, green trees and ground to meet it. It seemed simple enough and yet to reach the other side was an impossibility we knew we would never attain. It just looked as though it could go on and on for eternity. Just for fun we would sometimes try to run on foot to the point which looked like the end of the ground and the beginning of sky. We had many talks about the clouds and how we would like to stand on one of them.

One might think, life was simple for me, but for many children, these things are thought about, tried out and questioned. Perhaps you have had the question asked of you by your children "Why is the sky blue?"

Today I still look at the sky with wonder. At times it looks as though we are living in the confines of a bubble globe. We are contained in the atmosphere God has planned for us and yet it remains vast and something to explore by children and adults, astronauts and star gazers. It is a mystery; an imaginative creation of never ending curiosity. Is there life out there? Where does heaven begin? Do people walk around on a cloud? Do they get bored? Are there people who have gone on before us looking through the clouds down on their loved ones here on earth? Are they protecting us? Are their tears what we call rain? It all sounds a bit silly, but not to a young one. I have heard it all and questioned it myself.

We are naturally curious about all that is unknown to us, but we are fortunate to have a sure Word available through the Scriptures if we expose ourselves to its teachings. There were writers such as Mathew, Mark, Luke, and John. There were former persecutors such as Paul who came to know Christ. He not only lived for Him, but wrote to and visited the early churches to help them through trials, their growth in the knowledge of God and Christian responsibility. These compiled Scriptures are where we get our answers for those questions we ask ourselves and others about what and who is out there. Was there a creator that put all these things together with such precision?

Love as eternal as the vastness of the sky above is waiting to be accepted. I know now that God had it available for me because it is told of throughout the Bible from cover to cover. From the first verse in Genesis where it states "In the beginning God" to Revelation in the New Testament God's love is acted out for mankind. While looking up and into His world we see the never ending story unfolding before us of God reaching out of the vastness to all of us. Because of that great love so abundant and free we respond to the powerful reality of it. We find our place in His creation when we believe and obey His Word.

The door of acceptance is wide enough for anyone who will call on Him. He will walk with you through that door and show you His wonders.

Psalms 119:89 says "Your word, Oh Lord, is eternal; it stands firm in the heavens." We have a sky that seems as though it goes on forever, but better yet we have God's loving Word that is firm, sure, true and stands in the heavens, for us! It can be eternally yours. Isn't that wonderful?

SATISIFACTION

I was driving down our street to pull up to our house after a full day, when my husband met me at the bottom of our driveway with his car. "Jump in" he said. I was tired after a long day of meetings. I really didn't feel like getting out of my car to go somewhere else. He asked me to park my car and join him. Mark assured me that it would be a short trip and I would be back in no time at all. "Well O.K." He had to pick something up at the mall and he wanted me to go with him. We often do things together just because we enjoy each other's company so this wasn't a hardship. I slid across the car seat and away we went. Arriving at the Post Office behind the mall, I sat in the car and watched him go to another car with a set of keys and work the lock. I rolled down the window and asked what in the world he was doing? "That's someone else's car!" I thought he had lost it! He turned to me and opened my car door. With one motion he declared that it was my car now. Honestly, I said nothing. That is quite unusual for me. I got in and turned the key to follow him home in total

Love From Every Angle

silence. "What had he done?" You see, I have a passion for sports cars. Let me tell you that when I found my voice again, I said "Thank you."

Our son, Derek, and my husband, Mark, had been working on finding me a little car I would enjoy without my knowledge. I was thrilled. I felt as though they thought I was important enough to surprise with such a great find. I don't know who was more pleased, the giver or the receiver. We have had many wonderful rides in that car. Mark and I drove all the way up into Virginia and back in one day with the top down. It was so much fun. At night, in the summer months, we would take the little car out and ride as far as we could after our evening meal with the stereo up and the top down. We used it for our release vehicle. We solved the world's problems in that small space and felt all the better for it!

Why am I telling you this? It's a memory of love to me. The fact that Mark and Derek had been searching in the paper together, keeping their eyes and ears open showed father and son team work. Although it was a gift from my husband, our son, Derek, joined in the fun. It reminds me of 1 John 4:7a which tells us "Dear friends, let us love one another, for love comes from God. Also 1 John 4:11 says "since God loved us we also ought to love one another.

Thoughtfulness is an important part of giving to another. Thankfulness from the receiver should follow and enjoyment for all comes next. God in the same way set the example when he carefully and thoughtfully planned for mankind. He created the heavens and the earth and all that went in them. He had us in mind long before we were formed and planned for a relationship with us. This would include His son Jesus Christ and the Holy Spirit to intervene in our lives. We would have to respond to Him in acceptance of that love and a relationship would form. Problems would be solved and conversations in prayer that would include listening and talking would occur. The silence I mentioned would also be part of our relationship with God. That means we need to have a two-way conversation with our Lord, listening quietly to Him before we jump in to speak.

Digging in the Word of God for answers is like searching for something you want. In a similar way, Mark and Derek searched for just the right car to enjoy. God wants us to enjoy Him and be happy with the results of our search. It may seem tedious at times, but then suddenly you see what you have been looking for and the answer to the puzzle is solved. Let's all take from God's plan, the system He has worked out for us and use it.

Be thankful and rejoice in what you have found in the Savior Jesus Christ. Take advantage of the silence, the conversations in prayer and the listening. Your search will bring you to Him. The joy of knowing Jesus will fill your heart with new understanding of His love. It will bring to mind all that He has done for you and planned for your enjoyment while you serve Him here.

THE POTTER'S PIG

While visiting my brother-in-law in Connecticut, I had an opportunity to get away from the work we were trying to accomplish and shop for 15 minutes. "Oh stop here!" I recall saying, to my husband, "I'll be quick!" My husband, Mark, was driving and he and Brad were going to put gas in the car and pick up a few items we needed at the station. I, on the other hand, wanted to search the little consignment shop around the corner for a treasure to take back to North Carolina. I flew out the door with a yell of promise that I would not hold things up at all. "Just get your things done and I will watch for you. I'll be ready to jump in the car as soon as you pull in the drive." Well, he just had to trust me. There was much to do at Brad's and we were on a limited time schedule. I flew up the tiny staircase and opened the door. Oh, I love a little shop with thoughts of finding just the right thing to fill my heart with joy.

Looking around quickly, I could see that the front of the shop was filled with this and that and the back room was jammed with clothing items. I was not interested in the latter. I wanted an item or two that had a special look or meaning. As I perused the area, I could see there were furniture pieces to fix up and new items being priced at that very moment. I said "hello" to the ladies running the shop and found out the store had been owned by the family for a very long time. They quickly gave me a thumbnail sketch of its history. As we talked I saw a matching white soup tureen and gravy boat. I told them to put that aside for me as I continued to go through the various things with my eyes. Suddenly, a strange looking jug caught my attention. It was very plain with a cork in the middle of the top, an unfinished rim and a small handle on the side. It measured approximately 12 inches high and was ordinary looking with a putty colored glaze finish. I stared at it for a minute or two, but soon moved along to search out more interesting objects. As I tried to move on I kept coming back to this curious item. I had just a little time left, so I brought the jug down gently and walked over to the counter. "What is this strange looking piece?" I asked. As she began to tell me the history of this *Potter's Pig*, it suddenly went from ordinary to intriguing. When a potter finished his day's work of crafting beautiful plates, platters and such he would take the leftover clay and fashion a Potter's Pig. This served two purposes. First, no clay would go unused and second, a family would have a bed warmer at a very inexpensive price. The piece did not have to be fancy, with etchings and color as his other handy work, it just needed to be functional. This particular idea was a regular practice for a potter approximately

100 years ago. I knew that I had found my treasure! I paid the price, and ran out the door talking as I went. "You won't believe what I just found! You're going to love this story!" As we headed back to Brad's I relayed the tale and glowed inside. I thought it was an interesting picture of Christ!

The Potter was a master of his craft. He spent countless hours every day perfecting each item at the wheel. A mound of clay slapped onto the surface of the wheel began the creative process. His hands gently holding the clay and molding it with water and pressure, each precious piece was formed for the owner who would one day take it home to show it off and use it for his purpose. He repeated this ritual again and again making beautiful plates, bowls and cups. Then he would place each one on a rack to dry before painting and glazing. Each piece would be fired in the hot kiln to insure the finish and give it a glorious look. Some people were able to purchase these items while others could not afford such luxuries.

Years ago, houses were cold, but for a fire in the center of the house. Many had only that to keep the house warm. You can imagine the thrill it would be to bring home a Potter's Pig for the chilly sheets of the beds. I'm sure a father would be the one to fill it with boiling water and roll it across the covers before the little ones climbed into bed. It was heavy to begin with and the water would make it all the more weighty and hot. The original cork was still in the top of my Potter's Pig. Its rim around the top of the jug was unfinished and raw. I thought about that and knew that it represented me as a useful instrument in the hands of God.

We are all a work of art created by the Master's hand. Although some are showy and colorful, others are plain. All have an unfinished edge somewhere. We can be like that Potter's Pig and bring warmth to a home and a happy glow. I'm sure when the father filled the Pig the children cheered "Warm beds, Warm Beds!"

Before I was told what this funny looking jug was I knew it was something that was to be filled. Until we understand that we are loved by God, we are empty. God will fill our empty vessel with Himself and we can bring joy to others because of the Master's work. We all have an unfinished rim, meaning he is still working on us. Just because we are not famous or necessarily beautiful as others does not mean we cannot be used to bring hospitality to others and the good news of the love of God. Jeremiah 18:1-4 tells us that the master potter shapes the clay into what He sees best to do with it. We are all in His hands and He does with us as He wills. At the end of verse 6 of that same chapter we read "Like clay in the hands of the potter, so are you in my hand."

Do not wait until you think you are good enough like some well known person you admire. Let's be used just where we are in whatever capacity He chooses for us. A smile brings a good feeling to anyone, an arm around someone in need, or an encouraging word is as useful to God as boiling water is to a "Potter's Pig."

THE GIFT OF GOD'S FORGIVENESS

There is an issue that plagues the human soul. It's the problem of forgiveness. The measure of this subject is misunderstood by most of us because we have not absorbed the measure of God's forgiveness. We assume that God is like us, so we think, "I can't believe I did that! How can God forgive me, I can't forgive myself?"

We also find it hard to appreciate God's forgiveness when we think of Him as a perfect being somewhere out there far away in heaven. We dream of meeting Him one day when He gently takes us home to be with Him, perhaps when we are very old or very sick. All that surely seems to be a long way off as we make plans, work, and live life. We pray to Him, but it is difficult sometimes to sense His presence in our lives.

God seems distant until we become aware that we have sinned. Then we are in the position to meet God right where we are. We need Him at that moment and we need forgiveness for our sin. "Lord, help me!" we cry. "Lord forgive me, Lord straighten things out, please!"

God hears us in our desperation when we sincerely want *Him,* and not just relief from the problem that has been created. He supplies us with that which we need most...forgiveness.

God wants us to receive the forgiveness He so freely offers. He wants us to get beyond our guilt and accept His gift. It is free for the taking with no strings attached. It's often hard to understand, but that's what God promises.

Although God forgives us completely when we confess and repent, one of the biggest problems we have is that we cannot forgive ourselves. Sometimes we think, "OK, God forgave me but...I shouldn't have handled it that way." or "If I had just done this or that, things would have come out differently. I wouldn't be waking up in the middle of the night with regret." Perhaps we don't realize that God does not play games with forgiveness and *He* will not bring up confessed sins to us again and again.

Many times it is easier to understand God when we examine how He has treated others. King Manasseh of the Old Testament is a great example of a malicious sinner who confessed, repented, and received God's forgiveness. II Chronicles 33 and II Kings Chapter 21 recount the story of this historical king of the Southern Kingdom of Judah. He was incredibly sinful. He reigned over Jerusalem for fifty-five years from 697 to 643 B.C. In Chronicles 33:2 the Bible says, "He did evil in the eyes of the Lord." Manasseh was, according to the Scriptures, the most evil king Judah had ever had.

Manasseh had been raised by a godly father, King Hezekiah, yet King Manasseh became a complete contrast to his father. Manasseh introduced other religions to Judah that utterly perverted the worship of the one true God. Other kings had done evil things too, but King Manasseh's portfolio took wickedness to new levels. He sacrificed people, even his sons. He practiced sorcery, divination and witchcraft, as well as consulted mediums and spiritists. King Manasseh ignored God's law and diabolically led the nation to sin and violate God's covenant relationship with them. This strong willed King led the parade of hideous, sick behavior. He justly earned his reputation as the most wicked king in Judah.

There is, however, a lesson of encouragement for us in this story. God had made a promise to Judah that if they would worship Him and remain faithful to Him He would bless them. King Manasseh had driven his people astray into acts that shocked even the heathen of that time. God was deeply distressed by Manasseh's sin and that of his people, so He had to step in. II Chronicles 33:11 tells us that the Lord brought against them the army commanders of the king of Assyria. They took Manasseh prisoner, put a hook in his nose, bound him with bronze shackles, and took him captive to Babylon.

The Bible says, "In his distress Manasseh sought the favor of the Lord his God and humbled himself greatly before the God of his fathers." Did you catch that? Where was the turning point? Did

King Manasseh remember his father's devotion to the true God and desire it for his own life? Did his circumstances reveal his need? We don't know. But Manasseh sought forgiveness and God granted it. God also restored Manasseh to his kingdom.

God with all His power, had mercy on this most wicked king who had disgraced His name, defiled His temple, and led his people astray. Would God not do the same for us? There is always forgiveness for whatever sin we have committed when we humble ourselves before God and seek His favor.

Just as Manasseh had to face God and deal with his sin, so must each of us. Even though Manasseh was all powerful in his kingdom, he didn't get by with his sin and couldn't save himself. Although he had been very fortunate to have a father who followed God's ways, his faith could not excuse Manasseh from his own sinful acts. Each of us is responsible for our own sin. We can't hide it from God and we cannot save ourselves. We stand defenseless before God when our sin takes over and drives us to destruction. When we acknowledge our sin to God with humility, He will forgive us and restore us. John shares this great promise of God in I John 1:9, "If we confess our sins, he is faithful and just and will forgive us our sins and purify us from all unrighteousness." The LORD says in Isaiah 1:18, "Though your sins are like scarlet, they shall be as white as snow; though they are red as crimson, they shall be like wool."

All of us have committed sins we would not want to parade in front of anyone. We have hurt others, hurt ourselves, and we may have even led others away from God. The story of King Manasseh is a true story of restoration. Wouldn't you like for your story to be another true story of restoration? It is possible.

God in His mercy will hear you when you seek His favor, not just relief from the pain of your circumstances. God desires to restore you to fellowship with Him. Manasseh had to reach the point of having his kingdom taken away from him and being led away into captivity before he turned to God with a humble heart. What will it take for you to humble yourself and seek forgiveness?

God is waiting for you to come to Him. He longs for a right relationship with you. He desires to restore you to fellowship with Him. He is loving and tenderhearted to His children. He longs to wrap His arms around you and comfort your broken heart. He wants you to enjoy abundant life in Christ free from worry and guilt.

An old adage we've often heard is "forgive and forget." Maybe we don't always have to forget. It is good to remember God's gracious acts so that we know it was God who restored us. Remembering rather than forgetting has its merits. As mysterious as the act of receiving forgiveness is, through it God peels back love's reality bit by bit.

Yielding to God's ways we discover the many layers of His forgiveness toward us. Each time we receive His forgiveness reveals more of Christ. Thus, God's forgiveness whisks away the dirt that covers up the true picture of His grace.

King Manasseh was a proud and arrogant man who was humbled by God. While Manasseh thought he was in charge, he led a self possessed life. He had to be brought down to humiliating depths. Then he learned a valuable lesson, it is always best to do things God's way. It was a hard lesson to be sure, yet through it Manasseh found God's forgiveness and his relationship with God was restored.

Learn from Manasseh. When the Holy Spirit reveals your sin, humble yourself, confess, and repent. Accept God's forgiveness and move forward under God's direction. Forgive yourself. God already has. Don't drag around a regret or degrading memory like an old rag doll. Yesterdays are gone. Each day passes quickly, so live each moment fully, trusting God's love. Claim your future with God, a future with hope and assurance.

"I LOVE YOU THIS MUCH!"

When you love someone, it is often hard to put into words just how much your heart overflows with emotion to express that feeling.

I have a dear friend who knows just what I am talking about. Her name is Barbara. She has always had a positive personality and I would describe her as an encourager. She would just as soon run across town rather than have a confrontation with someone. She doesn't like being at odds with anyone and if she felt she had hurt your feelings she would surely own up to the fact and ask your forgiveness with humbleness of heart. This is a gentle loving human being.

During the Christmas season of 2006, Barbara suffered from severe headaches that landed her in the hospital. Our local hospital transported her to another larger teaching hospital in the area more suited to meet her needs. After much consultation and testing the diagnosis was said to have been a brain tumor. The next thing we knew they determined it to be a brain infection that had developed into an abscess. In a relatively short period of time, Barbara had declined in health to the point she was unable to walk, eat without assistance or read because of blurriness and double vision. Her mouth filled with sores from medication made speaking and eating so difficult. Her right side was completely numb. Determined to do all she was able, Barbara practiced writing her letters and forming sentences. Barbara's family had rallied around her exhibiting their loyalty and love beyond measure. Her multitude of friends helped with food for the family, cards and letters to Barbara and prayed often.

In times such as these we often wonder why God would allow such devastation in a life so dedicated in service to God. Barbara had, after all, been the Assistant Teaching Director to the Raleigh, North Carolina Community Bible Study. I had heard her speak many times and knew the amount of study she put into her lectures and weekly lessons. Everyone loves Barbara. What had happened to our dear sister? One of our prayer requests was that God would heal her and restore her completely. We were heartsick to see Barbara suffering. Each of us asked God for a miracle.

I am so happy to tell you the rest of the story. Although we sometimes think we decide what is best, God goes about doing His work and knows what needs we have and determines what He will do according to His plan.

Barbara is a prayer warrior and was committed to bringing the needs of others before the throne of

Love From Every Angle

God. Her desire is to have a life that counts for the Savior she loves so much. While we were praying for Barbara, she was taking prayer requests and lifting each of us up to the heavenly Father. When we pray, God moves in mysterious ways to bring about changes in our lives and grow our understanding so that we are able to accept the mystery of His will. What and how much we understand is yet to be determined, but are we giving God praise in the midst of our questions and uncertainty? It is easier to see things in the light of hindsight. Much of the time our faith is "not by sight". We do not know what is happening or what will be the end result. We pray and God works.

May 3, 2007 came and we had our Sharing Day at Community Bible Study. This is our end of year brunch with all the ladies that studied together over the year. It is a time to eat together and give witness and thanks for what we have learned. Our dear Barbara walked into the room using her walker! We were so thrilled to see her among us once again. Everyone wanted to touch her and speak with her and many did while we were still mingling before we settled down to pray and eat. At mention of her by our leader, Brenda, over 200 women stood to their feet. The applause was deafening. Barbara threw kisses as tears came to every eye including her thankful face. She expressed her "I love you this much" when she spread out her arms.

Just days before, we had learned that the latest MRI had shown the abscess gone and the swelling in her brain no longer there. What elation we all felt this day! The morning just got better and better. Toward the end of our meeting after many had shared their thoughts I watched Barbara being prepared with a tiny microphone attached to her lapel. As she stood up and held onto her walker, music began to play over the speakers. Was our beautiful alto going to sing? I was overwhelmed when she began to sing out "Talk About A Child Who Do Love Jesus" You could have heard a pin drop in the room. As she sang I thought of the many times I had heard testimony of God's healing powers. There was not a dry eye in that hall. Barbara smoothly transitioned into speaking to us with careful words. She walked us through her journey over the last 5 months with an emphasis on Jesus. She spoke of her husband and family with great love and appreciation. Barbara told us of her faith that sometimes wavered, of the foundation in Christ that shook, but never crumbled. Then she told us of her meditation on the Word of God in the dark times and recollection of verses memorized before she fell ill. She said she often sang songs in her heart when she was unable to voice them. Barbara thanked us for the many prayers and the faithfulness of God. She was the same Barbara, but changed in a way that was deeper and heartfelt. She had learned and grown in the valley. We have been amazed and awe struck with God's complex yet fruitful methods he chose to use in her life.

Although she still has no feeling in the right side of her body, Barbara remains faithful with a great attitude. You see, she said several months ago that "It is in times like these you find out whether or not what you teach about is real." How true. Many times it is when we have been put to the test, we find out whether or not our faith is grounded. Still in the healing process, Barbara knows God loves her abundantly. She stretched out her arms to show us. Barbara then said "I love Him and all of you this much too!" We all stood again with applause of thankfulness to our amazing God and gratefulness for the witness of God's love and grace extended to Barbara. We are proud to call Barbara our friend and sister and so thankful for the mentor she has been to us. We all said in unison "God is good all the time." What a blessing!

"Therefore I will praise you, O Lord, among the nations;
I will sing praises to your name." 2 Samuel 22:50

MISMATCHED

Talking with friends about various things and laughing at the way we were and what we have become always brings up the subject of those we have not seen in a long time. Those were the days, weren't they? We would like to forget some of them, but there are people we will have in our memory for a lifetime. The tall dark handsome unknown we watched each day while changing classes in school. The preppy popular girl we knew with everyone around her almost all the time. The outcasts and the hurt we saw on their faces when they were called cruel names and laughed at. Was all that temporary? It is surreal, but with us still in many ways. We are affected by the things that happen to us and in front of us no matter what the age. It makes us part of who we are. Were we liked? Were we rebellious and lazy? Have we got an image in our heads that is not matching reality? Maybe we have. The good news is that when we become connected to the Lord, He changes our image. We are now objects of His affection. Always having been loved by Him is a fact. Yet now we are His heir and His words and His actions mold and shape our new attitude and perspective. We have someone who loves us in spite of ourselves, our position, and even our physical appearance. Attractive, short and round, brilliant or average, in good standing or an outcast, He takes us on. Wrapping His loving arms around us, He gives us a new name, Christian. Now, we stand in a new place and walk with Him. We have access to His book, His wisdom, and His view. The treasures of His family are now ours.

At times, though, we fall back into talking sarcastically and gossip. Like Lot's wife, we long for our old life, looking over our shoulders at the things we used to enjoy. We act as though life with Him is not good enough. The Israelites are a good example. When rescued by God through Moses and living in the wilderness, they complained and longed for the fleshpots back in Egypt. They had cried out for God's deliverance, and when they received it, they complained about God's provision. Sometimes I am ashamed of the way we, objects of God's loving mercy, act. Dissatisfaction creeps in and makes us ask the question "How have you loved us?" as the Israelites asked in Malachi 1:2. That is arrogant audacity. Had they forgotten His demonstration of love for them throughout the years? Have we? Sometimes the events of our lives cloud the view of His protection, love and even deliverance. A look into the mirror of God's heart not only shows us His intentional love toward us, but reveals our inadequacies.

What do memories of yesteryear have to do with present day check points? God wants us to have a complete picture of our life through His eyes. It seems the older we get with more experience under our belt and time with Him helps in many ways. On our own we might think "I am a mess because of mistakes made in my past or injustices occurred that ruined my life." With great success we may think we haven't got real needs. That is why we need a corrected view through Christ. He puts things in proper proportion for us so that past experiences don't guide our life as much as His ways. In our life's journey with Christ we are getting a makeover. Each one of us needs a good look in the mirror of that love on a regular basis. It not only shows us who we are, but with His love reflecting through our lives, what we can be. The mirror of God's heart gives us a love look from every angle. We see how His plan has carried us to today as well as how it will take us to our future with Him. We get that forward and behind view. How can we question it? Why would we want to be without His love and slough it off as though it is dry and old? Are we reflecting the love given us in our new way of living now that we are one of His?

When God shows us our human weaknesses we need to pay attention to the guidance of His correction. He wants us to ask Him to help us with those things that keep us from acting like one of His grateful children. Bowing to His superiority and shepherd's heart leads us back to the right path. As God's children, we should show our love by appreciating the many forms in which His love comes to us. Sin though we will at times, it is still true that the Christian's life is "hidden with Christ in God." Colossians 3:3. That conjures up visions of a spiritual protective covering. We all ought to be thankful. " For I am convinced that neither death nor life, neither angels nor demons, neither the present nor the future, nor any powers, neither height nor depth, nor anything else in all creation, will be able to separate us from the love of God that is in Christ Jesus our Lord." Romans 8:38.

In God's mercy and kindness toward us He holds us close to Him where we are able to leave the past behind. We will not only be forward thinkers, but students learning to look ahead to God making a big difference in our lives.

It is important that you "Make it your ambition to lead a quiet life, to mind your own business and to work with your hands, just as we told you, so that your daily life may win the respect of outsiders and so that you will not be dependent on anybody." I Thessalonians 4:11.

I think we try to make things too complicated. Others may get the impression that to follow the Savior in lifestyle is way too much to ask. God encourages us to come to Him and He will do in us what we would never think possible. He helps us with knowledge of Him moving us to understanding, and finally wisdom. That puts knowledge and understanding into practice. This takes time with Him, and thankfully, He is long suffering.

CREATED INDIVIDUALS

A few summers ago I had an opportunity to take a car trip down to Orlando, Florida with our oldest daughter Kristen, her husband Rob, and our grandchildren, Lyndsey and Luke. Rob was interviewing with Wycliffe Bible Translators. Sitting with the kids in the back seat was a lot of fun. We told stories, played all sorts of games and just enjoyed each other's company. I was to help the children do their homework, make sure they were fed and spend time with them doing various activities. Kristen and Rob would be talking with the Wycliffe staff. When they were through interviewing, we visited Great-Gran in Merritt Island along with Lyndsey and Luke's cousins Kiah and Alex. After a few of the neighbors popped in to say hello, we were off to dinner with the children in tow.

What a wonderful time of talking and laughing with relatives! Although our time with them was short, it was memorable. That evening we were back in Orlando for rest, and another meeting with the interviewer for Rob and Kristen.

Love From Every Angle

Weeks later, back in High Point N.C. Kristen and I were talking in her living room when Rob came in the house with a package that had arrived from Wycliffe, Rob's new employer. As Kristen opened it and lifted the books from the box for Rob to read, she saw a small bundle of writing notes. "Oh Mom!" she said with excitement. "It's the woman on the wall." "What?" She stood up and sat next to me on the couch. She showed me a black and white print on the front of each note of a portrait showing a woman intently reading something on a few papers. Her head was draped with a white cloth and her face showed signs of wear from age and the harshness of life. Her hair was pulled back and out of sight. Dressed in black with a necklace of some sort, her mouth was slightly parted as if she were reading aloud.

What I most treasured about this vision were her hands. They were working hands. Instead of holding sick children, washing clothes or digging out a living, they held a message sent just for her. I tried to imagine the thought process going on in her heart and mind as she read God's Word.

You see, this was a woman in Papua New Guinea reading the Scriptures for the first time in her own language. She had never heard the incredible message of the Savior, the Son of God, who had come down from His position in heaven to be born of a virgin, and live among men. This same son, Jesus, taught a message of love and hope, with redemption for the sins of mankind. Dying, in our place, He took all our sins, discouragements, failures, and suffering upon Himself and allowed men of earth to beat Him, threaten and scourge Him for our sake. The most wonderful part of this true story is that Jesus arose on the third day after being put to death by the very people He came to save. God miraculously raised Him from the grave and He lives now to give us life. This interested woman was reading God's message of love to her. How wonderful to know there are people willing to bring this life giving message around the world.

As Kristen read the short explanation on the back of the note my eyes welled up with tears. It was hard to talk. I realized the thankfulness I have for the Savior and King who pays attention in detail to me and *all* His created individuals.

The photograph of the woman was taken by someone as she read God's Word in her native language. The missionary's daughter made the very large painting from the photograph. Using her own fingerprints to create the stirring image she emphasized how God's own imprint is left on our hearts through His Word. The original painting hangs on the wall of the Wycliffe headquarters in Orlando, Florida.

Just as the seeds of The Gospel, God's *Good News,* were planted in young Timothy of the New Testament through his grandmother Lois and his mother Eunice, they grew through the encouragement and mentoring of the apostle Paul, Timothy's spiritual father. Each of us who hear the Word of God and respond to Jesus in trust and obedience is given seeds of faith by God himself. We must exercise this faith to the fullest extent to love God as He loved us, with our whole lives and heart. He will water and fertilize these seeds for His work here on earth, for His glory and the spreading of The Gospel on rich soil. We must use what God has planted in our minds and hearts. God will reap the harvest.

Who knows whose life will be changed because they heard the truth? "This is love: Not that we loved God, but that he loved us and sent his Son as an atoning sacrifice for our sins." 1 John 4:10.

It is important that we pray for our missionaries throughout the world. They are on the front lines sharing the message of hope and love to millions who may never hear The Gospel if they did not go. Jesus was our example. He had compassion on all people and did whatever He could for the individuals in the crowds who followed Him. He taught in the synagogues and preached the Good News of the kingdom wherever He was. Turning to his disciples he said "The harvest is plentiful but the workers are few. Ask the Lord of the harvest, therefore, to send out workers into the harvest fields." Mathew 9:37-38.

THE SISTERS

Once in a while, you come across people that find their way into your heart forever. Meegie and Beth are two such women. Sisters, born seven years apart, they almost work as one. What one may start to say, the other finishes. When I speak of them, I tell others they are fun and real. They can bring down the house with their hysterical stories. So genuine are these sisters, one can find no pretense in their bones. They couldn't be more engaging. They will bring the heaviness or tension in a room to a halt and lighten its feel. Their closeness and love for each other is evident, as they sit together at functions and play off one another's words to the enjoyment of all. If you want to bring life and fun to a party, or heavy heart, invite "the sisters" and you are in for a good time. The most wonderful part of their interesting story is that their husbands get along as well as the sisters do.

One particular Sunday school morning, during our prayer time, the sisters announced that their father Carl D. Crawford, better known as C.D. would

Love From Every Angle

---

be moving in with Meegie and her husband, Bill. Meegie would be taking care of C.D. during his difficult time battling Parkinson's disease. We would not be seeing as much of her during this portion of C.D.'s care. Beth and her husband, Steve, would be close by to give her support and help if circumstances called for their intervention. Keeping C.D.'s anxiety to a minimum, and strength for Meegie was the sister's prayer. Beth would give Meegie breaks allowing her to attend church, periodically. Friends gathered around to hear what updates Meegie could give us on their father's condition.

February brought news of stomach cancer, adding to C.D.'s aliments. The sisters asked God to grant C.D. a pain free time. He was frightened and uneasy about the pain of death he may have to undergo. Wonderfully noted, C.D. never had to take one pain pill.

My husband, Mark, and I were out of town the first week in May when the news came. The sister's father had passed on. The funeral was very uplifting. I thought of the family often and prayed for peace as well as their return to church services and Sunday school.

Yesterday, during the church service, I caught a glimpse of Meegie. Excited to see her, I nudged Mark and told him that I spotted her in the crowd. During our Sunday school class we were recipients of a beautiful testimony Meegie and Beth gave of their family taking part in the passing of a loved one.

Their father stopped speaking on the Saturday three weeks prior to this date. His time was nearing for his departure from earth. Family gathered and they began to sing. Each family member from young to old piled onto the double bed he loved, with their beloved elder. What a picture! Holding one another's hands, they sang out the words to familiar hymns. They started with "Blessed Assurance." This was C.D.'s favorite hymn. Next they sang "Turn your eyes upon Jesus." After two days of not a word from him, they believe they witnessed their father get a view of heaven, for Carl opened his mouth to speak the words "Hallelujah, precious Jesus." The family had witnessed a wonderful transformation take place. The anxiousness on his face was gone now, replaced with a peaceful countenance. The last song for Carl was "Heaven is a wonderful place." What a memory for his children and grandchildren!

There are many times when loved ones die due to an illness or accident and it is extremely pain filled. Somehow, the long drawn out circumstances surrounding the event or the shock of their absence takes its toll on the entire family. There can be vivid memories of their struggle that fill our hearts so with sorrow. Often it is hard to shake off and we must go through the arduous journey feeling the loneliness of loss. I must say that Meegie and Beth taught us a lesson about handling a death in the family with dignity and hope.

C.D. and his wife loved the Jewish people. The couple supported them with their finances and prayer. In 1983 Mr. and Mrs. Crawford made a trip to Israel. While they were there, they purchased several "widow's mites." Meegie opened her coin purse in front of the class that day and told us the reason he carried these tiny coins. He wanted others to understand that we should not only give financially to the work of the Lord, but like the widow, we need to give our all to Jesus. Beth humorously chimed in. "As long as you have one of these you will never be in want!" Meegie passed a coin to each of us who had prayed for their father, as a gift from C.D. I will treasure it always.

As I watched and talked with the sisters I realized their depth. The joy they brought others came from the Lord and I interpreted it as strength of heart that only Jesus gives.

Just as Ezra in the book of Nehemiah of the Old Testament chapter 8:10 told the Israelites when he read them the law that "This day is sacred to our Lord. Do not grieve, for the joy of the Lord is your strength." I saw, in the sister's lives, the joy our Savior gives us through a life of service that is dedicated to Him. They had taken the Scriptures and worked them into their heart's soil. In the 12th verse of chapter 8, the Israelites were able to stop their grieving and serve others with joy because "they now understood the words that had been made known to them." Meegie and Beth have a relationship with Jesus that enabled them to put the death of their father in perspective. God gave Meegie and Beth joy in "the doing" for their Father in heaven as well as their earthly father. The light in their eyes was the evidence.

Are you ready for whatever the Savior may have for you? We never know what the future may have in store for us. Will you have to care for a dying family member? We learn from the Scripture, the lives of others and our own experiences. Is He preparing you for a special service? If you are His child He is making you fit for service. Are you searching to find what God has for you? Everyday life will give you plenty of opportunities to serve Him. The sisters had been prepared long before their father's passing for the strength and patience to care for him. Whatever He has in store for you, He is preparing you for it today. Thank Him today for His days of preparation that will give you the grace, knowledge and strength for service to Him.

UNDER WATCHFUL EYE

When arriving home one summer afternoon, I pulled into the driveway in my car for the uphill climb. It was bright that day and I was feeling good. Coming home to an empty house didn't bother me. I was in a great mood.

Although I was not expecting a visitor, I had one sitting on the ground at the top of the driveway straight ahead. Little as he was I stared at him and felt amazed. "Is that an owl?" I asked myself. I very gingerly opened the car door so as not to disturb this small friend who had come to call. Tiny and perfectly formed with feathers intact I was looking at a young Eastern Screech Owl called a Red Morph or a very young Great Horned Owl. I wasn't quite sure. He was alone and my motherly instincts urged me to stay near and watch carefully after him. He was adorable and I wanted to share my experience with whomever I could reach. Looking around I saw no one outside. "I can't leave, I thought, something might happen to this vulnerable creature." Aha! My neighbor across the street just pulled into her drive with her friend.

Love From Every Angle

Moving far enough away, I then shouted for them to come over quickly and see the small bird.

I felt so special and responsible at the same time. While my friend and her companion were with me I called my daughter, Britt, and told her about my find. She in turn called the animal service to come pick up the young bird so that it would have the best chance for survival. Alone and waiting for them to come to my address, I grabbed a camera and stretched out on the ground for a photo shoot. As if posing for a magazine layout, the tiny 7 or 8 inch owl turned his head and blinked his large gorgeous eyes as I took picture after picture.

Could it be while taking responsibility for the creature I was actually getting in the way? I may have been preventing the mother owl from rescuing her child. Perhaps he had fallen out of the nest during a flying lesson and his mother was testing his adventuresome spirit. I thought about this and wondered if she had been watching me from a nearby branch. Perhaps she thought of me as the enemy and her little one the prey. I dared not pick the young one up for fear that his relative might zoom down on me and misunderstand my intentions. So I made a judgment call. It was time for me to step out of the picture. The professionals would be here and they would take care of things. I thought if the mother saw that I was gone perhaps she would feel that it was safe to swoop down and intervene. I went into the house and tried to make as little noise as I could. Stepping away was the best thing I did. Perhaps the mother did indeed come to aid her own. I had not stayed where

I was able to witness the exact results of the next 10 minutes. I thought it was best to let nature take its course. When I returned to the window I did not see the owl anywhere. I quietly stepped out the door and took a quick look around. Perhaps there had been a family reunion in some low tree branches.

Nature can teach us so much about ourselves. There is a time to be nurturing and caring as well as a time to be protective and a time to let go. We all watch our children and should be there for them no matter how old they get. A mother's instincts never go away. Knowing that we cannot always be physically near, we are near in heart. My heart went out for this small bundle. I found myself looking around for its mother and thinking this bright eyed beauty was all alone. Until I trusted in the natural course of things, she may never have felt comfortable to come to his aid. He was not injured, just small and vulnerable to the elements. I imagine his mother was watching out for him all the time. I convinced myself that I had driven up moments after he appeared at the top of the driveway in the grass. This noisy human disturbed his activity and may have annoyed his mom.

As written in Ecclesiastes 3: 1 "There is a time for everything, and a season for every activity under heaven." It could have been that I was used for an adjustment period. If that is so, I am glad.

"Use me Lord for whatever cause you give me. Then, Lord, give me the intuition to know when it is time to get out of the way. You alone know best." Whether it is a bird that teaches me this lesson or my own dear children, may I listen to your voice and know when the timing is right to serve in a pleasing way or step back."

IT'S ONLY A SCRATCH

While helping sand the baseboards in my grandchildren's bedroom, my index finger slid along the carpet tack beneath. "Ouch!" I felt my body say. It hurt and bled, but I went into the bathroom, washed my finger and kept on working. This project just had to get completed! I was a little more careful with my movements this time. When my husband came home from work that evening we went upstairs to continue to do everything we could to move the room closer to the finish line. Haddon, our *in town* grandson, needed a place to call his own at Grandma and Appa's home. Luke and Lyndsey, our Pennsylvania grandchildren, would be coming for a visit in July. Wouldn't it be nice to have this room fixed for them all? We did finish most of the room, and now we would have to choose a carpet and make window treatments. I would continue to work on the one hundred year old bed my husband and I purchased in Maine that had belonged to one of the oldest men in Thorndike. Having layers of peeling paint on it, I would get that down to a workable smoothness and paint the bed a pleasing color. By this time I was watching my finger swell and felt the throbbing pain. I soaked it in hydrogen peroxide everyday and used an antiseptic ointment, all to no avail. A few more days went by, and the first joint began to ache as well as the other fingers on that hand. Our friends from Florida, Bob and Linda, were coming for a visit. There were errands to run and lots to do before they arrived. I thought I could take care of this tiny problem, but it seemed beyond me as the days went by. Four days out, I merely held my finger away from any bump it might get and complained to my husband. He said, "Go to a doctor, and don't tell me." I was insulted! Looking for a little sympathy, this didn't sit well with me.

This fourth day was very busy as well. Our company from Florida was to arrive around 3 p.m. I had responsibilities of my own to take care of before their arrival, and needed to go to the pharmacy for my mother. I asked the pharmacist to take a look at my finger, and told her what I had been doing for the cure. Her one remark was "Go see a doctor, that's really bad!" That sounded like Mark! After delivering Mom's medicine, I drove over to the emergency care clinic next to our local hospital. They saw me immediately. My finger was so tender, I was leery about letting anyone touch it, let alone squeeze it. They did neither, thankfully. The doctor's recommendation was to give me a tetanus shot, numb my finger, lance it and administer oral antibiotics. I was so worried about the pain of the procedure that I almost walked away with just antibiotics. Rational thought helped me realize what was right and what would help speed along the healing process. After some hesitation, I agreed to let them give me the most aggressive plan. Surprisingly, I did very well and was happy that I had gone through with the doctor's full recommendation. It was over in a matter of minutes. My husband and my friend, Linda, came in the door just as they were bandaging me up. It would be more than two weeks before I would have my finger feeling better and looking normal again.

This same story is true of sin in our lives. We assume that we can cover over or fix it with topical treatments. We may think it is just a scratch in an otherwise fine record. Sin is no surface matter. Straightening our posture and holding our head high is not the recommended solution as far as God is concerned. He is not fooled, nor will He be mocked. God is not winking at our sin. Sitting in that doctor's office, I knew that there would have to be drastic measures taken with this infected wound. Isn't that how sin has to be dealt with? It causes a flare up as if to tear at the very heart of God. He is grieved and we feel the resulting pain of our sin's harmful results. The deceiving thing about sin is that the first offense doesn't necessarily appear serious. A washing of our hands in the sink such a Pontius Pilate in Mathew 27:24, clears our conscience and we foolishly believe we are innocent of a crime against Jesus and should be able to keep on going. Time moves on, and we find ourselves swollen with a festering infection. Sin has had a beginning and it has taken hold. There is only one way to rid ourselves of this enemy of our soul. It must be dealt with or it will continue to destroy our lives, and the way we handle things. Our relationship with God has drifted. We are suffering. Proverbs 24:33 says "a little sleep, a little slumber, a little folding of the hands to rest." We cannot be lazy with sin. We cannot ignore the havoc it is wreaking on our person. Do not be fooled, as I was and think you can handle things yourself. Sin must be lanced, cleaned out and given the antibiotic of the Word of God and fellowship with Him and His family of believers. The Great Physician has the solution and the cure for our broken and festering hearts and lives. Take the doctor's advice and go with the most aggressive plan. You may be left with a scar of remembrance that teaches us to deal with this thing quickly in order to bypass the pain and suffering of willful avoidance. The blood of Jesus Christ cleanses us from all sin. He and He alone can fix our problem. 1 John 1:7 tells us that "the blood of Jesus his Son, purifies us from all sin." and 1 John 1:9 says "if we confess our sins, he is faithful and just and will forgive us our sins and purify us from all unrighteousness."

THE TREASURE BOX

Have you got a treasure box? Perhaps your grandfather lovingly made one for you when you were a child. You might have found an interesting looking box in which to keep those things you value most. At the moment, mine is an antique humidor. The things I would not want to part with are held inside this humidor with memories and stories of how I acquired them. It is getting full and my items are crowding one another. Soon I will be on the look out for a larger, more suitable container to place my valuables in. I think everyone should have a unique box. It is important to have a special place for your treasured things. I am a big proponent of keeping an item of a loved one and connecting it with a memory of great times, relationships and the story behind it. We are not always near our relatives anymore and there are not many who keep a diary of the events in their lives. This box and its contents make interesting conversation when talking about one's background. There are stories for friends and those in our family curious about what we did and who we met in our

Love From Every Angle

lives. Each item brings understanding of ownership to a special piece and listeners are given a glimpse of our history. Everyone likes to hear about times of adventure and some enjoy hearing about the sentimentality of attachment.

I am reminded of Jem's box in the fictional classic <u>To Kill a Mockingbird</u> by Harper Lee. Each item held a special meaning for the son of a 1930's tenacious lawyer. In those times when he was alone reflecting, he would take out the box that held the items he found in the hollow of a tree. With childlike wonder Jem was in thoughtful contemplation.

While reading in II Corinthians chapter 4 I noticed that Paul was telling the immature church that God puts His treasure in earthen vessels. That meant that His precious loved ones, we who trust in Him, are His treasure box holding the first of God's deposits, the Holy Spirit. God is the gift giver. He first gave us life through acceptance of His son's death and resurrection in our stead for our sins. In that moment, we were given the Holy Spirit to reside within our heart to go with us wherever we are. Paul explained to the people of that time, as well as ours in II Corinthians chapter 5: 5 that the deposit of the Holy Spirit was the guarantee of His presence and one's future.

Years ago people kept their treasures in clay jars. They were quite common in the Ancient Near East and I would imagine at least the head of the household had a clay jar of their own which was used for this purpose. God wants us to understand that we are given the Holy Spirit while living on earth. We then are a valued vessel, a treasure box holding the Spirit of God. That is an incredible thought. Our bodies are used for a wonderful purpose.

In Genesis chapter 1, we read that following the creation of heaven and earth the first thing that God spoke into being was light. Before we know God in a personal way we live in darkness. We have a veil covering our understanding of God. We cannot see His purpose although we may try to live the best lives we can under rule of our own conscience. Yet, as good as we try to be we are still working in darkness and there is no regenerated life and light present. For some, a wonderful thing happens. We hear about the sacrificed Savior who died in our place for our sins. We learn that God raised Jesus from the grave after three days in the ground and He lives now and forever to give us life. With the power of God and His power only, we are able to recognize the truth. Out of love for what He did for us we make our commitment to Him. God has loved us so much and God wants us for His own! We can be His and spill over with the light that is Him in us! What a concept!

I recall a story in Judges Chapter 7 of the Old Testament. The Midianites had taken over the Israelites' land. Gideon was the leader of the Israelites that God would use. He told Gideon to take only 300 of his men in order that Israel could not boast of victory in her own strength. They were then given trumpets and clay jars with torches inside them. Stealthily they made their way down to the valley where the Midianites were camped out. Now the Israelite's lights were hidden in the clay pots, but when the time was right Gideon told them to break their jars, let their light shine and blow their trumpets.

The fact is that although the torches represented many more soldiers than the 300 men that Gideon had with him, the ruse fooled the Midianites. God was the true power behind the clay jars. In us He is far greater than any army. The Midianites, who were so many in numbers that they could not be counted, turned on each other. In their confusion they fled and the Israelite's land was restored to them.

God wants us to be used by Him. We are cracked and broken from the darkness we lived in. I like the image of broken vessels because we all have frailties and cracks in our lives. It is when the Savior mends our broken lives and fills those cracks with His love that we can reflect His character and love to the world around us. He strengthens us while we are here learning and serving Him on earth. He can now use us for mighty works wherever we go. His treasure in us is then manifested to others. The inner treasure is what gives us strength and courage to share Him with the world. Just like the light God first gave the world, it is the first thing He gives a believer, the light of awakening to Him and the realization of our pitiful weak attempts of living without God. He helps us see our need for Him. We need His light living in us. It is real. It fills the dark voids of our heart. We will think differently, talk differently and our aim will be to serve the Savior through eyes of hope, hands to help and minds to learn more of Him. We are the treasure box, this human vessel with the indwelling of the Holy Spirit. Regenerated beings still marvel at the miracle of redemption that allows this to take place and enjoy telling anyone who wishes to know about it.

My old humidor has a story that speaks of the purpose it served. Now it is in my hands and it has a new purpose. The items inside tell stories of their own. Each item tells of loved ones past and present who handed their treasures on to me. I will meet some of them again in the future of eternity. Until I do, I will hold those items, wear some, and remember the people who mean so much to me. This earthen vessel we live in will continue to be guided and taught by the Holy Spirit. We are God's container that will continually give witness to the story of love flowing from the infinite God extended to a fallible human. I will give thanks for this gift passed on to me. One day I will see the beaming face of my indwelling God.

SHAPE AND FORM

We have a lot of trees here in North Carolina. Friends from other regions of the country have mentioned that our woods are dense. We still have an abundance of trees in the city of Raleigh. This is wonderful because our fair capital is constantly growing and building to accommodate an ever booming population. It remains beautiful as residents for the most part take good care of their properties. The main thoroughfares are creatively landscaped and filled with flowers and lovely shrubs rather than litter.

The trees always delight me. In spring I love looking at the different colors and shapes of the trees that form a backdrop for the flowers and bushes. There is that lovely light spring green of new leaves against the dark evergreens and the lavender blooms of the Eastern Redbud as well as the white pear trees, azaleas and pink dogwood. It is a continual parade of newness of another season of beginnings. Each year it comes around again it is as though I am viewing it for the first time. My husband and I always make a game of pointing out the new buds and colors of spring as we travel down the highway. In the spring and summer I get real industrious planting in my garden to add to its variety. Then there is fall, the time for bulb planting. We see bright yellow bushes popping up all over the city, red maples, shrubs of purple and gold again against the evergreens. It is spectacular! The cool days are filled with memories and activities that include pumpkins, family and the Farmer's Market. I always feel as though I can breathe better in the crisp air. We shop for berries and gourds as well as orange and white pumpkins. If the children are available, I take the grandkids and let them pick out these items. I have a pumpkin for each of them to be represented whether they are living in town or not, on our front steps outside our home. We all know pumpkins are a child's delight. Last, there is winter. The leaves have fallen, we're wearing coats and gloves, the sky is a grey-blue and the grass is brown. Many people may think this is our dreary season, but I love the trees during this time about as much as when they are fully dressed in their wonderful array of leaves and flowers making them appear as if adorned in ballroom gowns. I study their shape and form with great fascination. I like the dusk time of day and even an hour or two after. When it is darker outside the sky makes the bare trees stand out, displaying each unmatched silhouette. My imagination is brought out as I see what they are truly made of. Years of wind, drought, sun, rain, and storms have grown them either strong and straight or weak and bent. I am able to see the structure of their priceless beauty. During this season I have often told my husband I like them in a unique way because I can see what holds the leaves in place. A gnarled knot in a trunk makes me think that something leaned against the tree with great weight while it was growing or worse, it has a disease. I am sure it was not like that as a young seedling. Could it have been damaged during its years of growing? Most of the time though, I will notice that its branches are rising toward the sky as if to say, "I am here and happy in it, have you noticed me? Darkness doesn't bother me. I am at peace." The moon seems to compliment the trees and the stars are their accompaniment.

Isn't this true of you and me? After years of growing into ourselves we have a place to stand and be either strong in our place or damaged by the weather of life. God made these trees as well as he made us. Each has a personality of its own, a unique way to represent our kind. Both trees and humans need good soil and roots to grow deep to give us security and strength to withstand the throws of life.

We can learn so much from observing trees. How are *we* when all is laid bare? When the facade is gone and we are what we are, in spite of all the circumstances? Have we reached up to God as if to shout "I love you Lord!" Have we dug deep into His Word and searched for food and the fertilizer of truth and knowledge for our growth? Will our little ones be able to sit in our lap, as a child in a strong tree and glean from our security in Christ? Think of this when you plant your next tree or have a child join your family and depend on you. You should be the

Love From Every Angle

strong tree with God's help. They are the seedling depending on your protective branches.

Enjoy every season of life with the heavenly Father who made and cares for you and yours. Even trees need rain as well as sunshine and winds to strengthen their roots and trunk. We need everything that comes our way by God's appointment. Receive it and lift your head, praising the heavenly Father for making you the way He has. As your life develops, what shape will you be in? Trusting in your Maker with pure joy through trials will mature you so that you will develop perseverance as explained in James chapter one verses 2-6. It will help you withstand the tests in life keeping you from being tossed like a wave of the sea because you have doubted. Shape and form that pleases Him will occur as you grow in wisdom as well as leadership in His kingdom. I think of doubting as a tree trunk with a sucker on it. It weakens the tree and until it is cut off, the main trunk is unable to build real strength for the life of the tree. John 15:5 says "I am the vine; you are the branches, if a man remains in me and I in him, he will bear much fruit; apart from me he can do nothing."

THE LITTLE THINGS

Life is full of everyday dos and don'ts. Each day has its own agenda. Although we may or may not acknowledge them, they are there and lurking around every corner with watchful eye prodding and poking our conscience. We go about acknowledging or ignoring the things that need attention.

I have many memories of fun and laughter in my childhood. Life was happy and loving most of the time. My parents always put family first and our home was a refuge for the hurting or out of work. As young and impressionable children this was good for us to see and experience in our home. We learned that putting others ahead of selfish pleasure was important and a key ingredient in the development of our character.

We lived in a tiny house, perhaps 1400 sq. ft. It sat on 1 acre of land. It had a large kitchen that also served as a dining room as well. The working area was at one end and the table with two leaves was at the other with a picture window. It was almost always filled with our family as well as extended family and friends. We laughed and laughed around that table. Someone always had a joke and especially a great story to tell. The adults told about life when they were kids with their parent's relatives. We little ones stayed seated even after the meal had ended and listened to them go on and on. We'd ask them to repeat our favorite stories and they would elaborate and exaggerate for our enjoyment. When they were intense, we children were intense and when they laughed we did too with sheer delight. I loved the stories! I watched each adult's expression and thought they were wonderful.

One day without notice my Aunt Dot arrived. She was my mother's oldest sister. I saw she had a lone suitcase and was smoking like a factory chimney. She was a small woman and was unusually quiet this visit. Mom got her settled and they talked into the wee hours of the night at the table in the kitchen. My sister, Dale and I shared a room and were safely tucked in for the night. Dad stayed up for a while, but had to get to bed, because he was working various shifts on the Connecticut State Police Force. Weeks went on as Aunt Dot stayed. Her visit turned into a few months. Mom and she talked on and on. The coffee was always on the stove. There was a grown-up thing going on of which my sister and I were not a part. We just bounded in and out of the house and enjoyed the family.

Early after breakfast on a weekend after her long visit with us I joined my aunt as she packed her suitcase, open on the living room floor. She talked sweetly and softly to me. I noticed she was putting a large Bible in her suitcase with her other things. I don't think I will ever forget that moment. The morning sun was shining in the large window, at a right angle to the fireplace in the room. There was something different about that new day. "What are you doing?" I asked. I guess I thought she would stay with us forever, but it was just a temporary visit until the storm in her life passed. She hadn't come with a Bible, but she left with one. All the days and nights had been filled with talks and love from my parents. You see my Aunt Dot had realized she was lost.

My mother and father had found real meaning for their lives not too long before her arrival. God had let them in on His provision. They had a new direction and meaning in life. They were not only just good people anymore. Mom and Dad belonged to God through belief in Him. They passed the truths of Scripture's love and forgiveness on to Aunt Dot and told her she too could find true meaning as well as peace in her tumultuous life. She finally believed Jesus was meant for her as well. Admitting she had need and that she was a sinner, as we all must come to know, she had bowed her head and talked with the God she only had made reference to when exasperated or holidays came around.

As the two of us knelt down by her suitcase and I watched her pack, she told me that she knew the Savior in a personal way now. Things were going to be different. She realized who He really was and He loved her. She would be reading His Word. My parents had given her a Bible. It was a moment to remember. Mother had not made a big deal out of

Love From Every Angle

---

it but as I remember, there was a new and stronger bond between the sisters. All the events in life were looked at in a new light. They had Jesus to talk about and share now. During subsequent visits I witnessed conversations of hope and encouragement. Nearing 8 at this point in my young life, there would be a lifetime of growth and lessons to learn. I too, would come to the realization that all mankind needs the Savior.

To talk about the little things in life which make us stronger and bring lasting pictures to mind, is to tell you *this* particular story. I witnessed lives changed again and again in our little home. It was perhaps our most memorable home of those we lived in as I was growing up. Not only my aunt, but cousins, friends and other family members heard of the saving life of Christ in that home. Snapshots of family and love in my memory, has been a shaping and molding influence that has remained with me to this day.

Long before I ever knew it, before I was born, God was lining up situations and people for my experience here on earth. At the proper time, God would reveal Himself to me. Through the Bible I was raised with and all that was available through Him, God shaped the events of my life to give me an awareness of His son Jesus Christ and a desire to know Him.

Why remember this seemingly little thing? As if watching a black and white movie I see her arms packing with Bible in hand and remember her peaceful facial expression. Why do I remember my mother's kitchen and all the people who slept on our couch over the years? I don't know, except to say

God uses everything in our lives and His Word for our understanding. He uses them to pique our interest in spiritual matters.

Never think that the little things in life are unimportant in a child's eyes. They observe and know early on what and where our priorities are. As Christ is our example, we are theirs and our words and actions will guide them to knowledge of Him. They are like little sponges and soak up everything around them. While they are young and their hearts are tender, nurture them and put God first for His sake, your sake and the sake of your little ones.

> "Train a child in the way he should go, and when he is old he will not turn from it."
> Proverbs 22:6

SHOW ME WHAT TO DO

There isn't a single human being that has lived on this earth without difficult situations to work through. Sometimes these difficulties seem to come in bunches and spread over a period of years. Life just goes on and on with one thing after another. Friends have been there, but that doesn't seem to make a large difference to the one experiencing trials. When it is you dealing with ongoing problems it is hard to see anything but this enormous obstacle blocking any positive influences or thoughts. You may feel heavier in your shoes causing you to barely step one foot in front of the other. While others are talking about shopping, swimming at the pool with the family or refinishing antiques, you can barely make it through the conversation for the deep pressure you are experiencing. The person you are conversing with might as well be saying "blaa bla bla bla blaa." Your mind is stayed on a desperate search for relief. This intense period of time is perhaps the hardest thing you have gone through so far in your life. Who hears your heart's cry? While life goes on so sweetly for some, you, my friend, are dying inside. Life now seems stationary and the depth of feeling *alone* follows you and tries to break through your circumstance to confuse you into thinking there is no one who understands, no one who knows, and no one who can possibly see the pain you are in. No doctor can prescribe a cure and no friend can hear enough and soothe the broken heart that weighs heavy in your chest. Frustration, and Doubt, its twin, want their way. They walk arm in arm marching toward you in hopes they will now reign on the throne of your heart and paralyze your Christian effectiveness. Their commander, God's enemy, Satan, has given his orders. Frustration and doubt have visualized their mission and they are now on their way to carry out defeat and depression.

Have I painted a picture you can recognize? It is a common one for sure, and everyone has been in a valley if they have any years on them at all. Life in many ways teaches us that lessons are often learned in the valley and celebrations erupt on the mountaintop. Yet we walk in the valley during hard times. These tough situations are God's battleground, where he does His best work. He has laid the foundation to take down the enemy at Calvary. This is where hope is given to the hopeless, the weak, the weary and the distressed.

We know that life is not always as carefree as a child's game; it is a battle with a series of training and conditioning tactics that will help us overcome with God's power and direction.

Satan's war tactics are to work on our emotions. He massages them, stretches them, and manipulates.

He plays on time and worry. He knows that we are concerned with when this trouble we encounter will end. He wants us to think God will not come through and save the day or our loved one. He loves insecurity. Will God provide? Is He able? We need to understand this. Satan is no match for God! Although things may seem hopeless and unfixable at times, God is still on His throne and ruling with great might. There will never be anyone to unseat Him nor hinder His plans. As Job stated in Job 42:1 and 2 "I know that you can do all things; no plan of yours can be thwarted." Did Job know something we do not? Having gone through the horrific ordeal of losing family members, his livelihood and health he had a stronger understanding in his heart. He came through with the knowledge that circumstances, friends, evil pressures and war itself can be used of God in our lives. Job said again in that same chapter that "my ears had heard of you but now my eyes have seen you." (Job 42:5).

We must trust that God has given us everything we need for the battle. We have His perfect love. "Perfect love drives out fear" according to 1 John 4:18. That simply means if we are consumed with fear, then we don't understand God's perfect love for us. Grab hold of it. Be mindful that He found you and supports you in all areas of your life.

As in all armed forces we are given a commander, a manual, regulations to follow and repetition in training so that when the battle is raging we have all we need, including our fellow Christian soldiers to help remind us of the weapons at our disposal. So many times in the midst of the storm, confusion has made its home in our minds. We feel overwhelmed and want to pull the covers over our head and hopefully go to sleep until the tempest passes. That cannot be allowed. Satan would have us angry, discouraged and fretful. He'd love it if we lost sight of the goal. My friend, we have the Savior who would do anything he can to help us not only get through our situations, but come out victorious! He is the head commander who knows the enemy's tricks and supplies us with His truth, His strength, His courage and might, prayer and a shield of defense. He tells us to recall His mercies, His kindness and all the times He has delivered us from the snare of the evil one. In Isaiah 41:10 God says "So do not fear, for I am with you; do not be dismayed, for I am your God. I will strengthen you and help you; I will uphold you with my righteous right hand." It's all about trusting Him for the great times and the hard times.

Sometimes we take a wound to the heart and it seems as though it will kill us. I have felt the hurt and sometimes lost a fight. Tears flow and sleep does not come. God heals our broken heart when we yield to His ways in life's struggles. I have heard that it is important to choose your battles. That is not the way it works in life. I say, just choose God. We are not alone. God goes to battle with us. At times we think it is all about the situation when in fact, it is truly all about learning God's ways. Learn to be consistent, deliberate, to react according to training. Pray, and repeat His words by memorizing Scripture. When the time comes to go to battle, those things will be with you. All you need do is look to your commander as you hear Him speak to your heart and respond entirely to all that God shows you to do.

BEAUTY IS FLEETING

When we are very young and full of life we are blessed with lots of energy, bright eyes, and kissable cheeks. Hair is full, and flowing. Sure of one's self, there is little need for make-up. The figure, being slender, is one that can laugh in the face of candy. Little sleep never seems to bother. This straight walking, confident youth tosses her locks as if she just won a spot in a shampoo commercial.

Then, if we are blessed, children enter our lives. With them, we take on responsibilities for their care and nurturing along with other responsibilities of bill paying, career, house repair, pets, committees, friends and the many situations in life. Time passes by quickly and after our children are grown and successful and grandchildren and great-grandchildren are working their way through school and starting families of their own, we notice the body suffers the normal aches and pain effects of years of wear and tear. The old and once firm body just isn't the same. Pull-ups and slip-ons replace fashion trends. The locks of curls atop your head begin to thin out and some are left with a wisp of a not so recent past. The bow in your hair as a child is now used at your neck to hid sags and winkles.

Thankfully, God has the answer. We may be falling apart on the outside but the inside, if we are faithful, is being renewed every day. 11Corinthians 4:16 says, "Therefore we do not lose heart. Though outwardly we are wasting away, yet inwardly we are being renewed day by day." He knows our human frailties and weaknesses and loves us through all stages in life. He gives us armor from head to toe and makes sure that if we trust Him, we will be clothed in it. As stated in Ephesians 6:13 He wants us to, "put on the full armor of God, so when the day of evil comes, you may be able to stand your ground, and after you have done everything, to stand." Wobble though we may, as we age on the outside, God doesn't want us to worry about our balding head, corn sore feet or our not-so-trim waistline of youth. He asks in verses 14-18 of the same chapter that we "stand firm then, with the belt of truth buckled around your waist, with the breastplate of righteousness in place, and with your feet fitted with the readiness that comes from the gospel of peace. In addition to all this," He asks us to "take up the shield of faith, with which we can extinguish all the flaming arrows of the evil one. Take the helmet of salvation and the sword of the Spirit, which is the Word of God. And pray in the spirit on all occasions with all kinds of prayers and requests. With this in mind, be alert and always keep on praying for all the saints."

When we feel too tired to do much of the physical work we were able to do as a youth, we know that we have a God who will continue to supply us with everything needed for our journey on earth. Though it becomes harder in the winter of life, we can make use of our slower days and be strong in prayer, communing with our God in ways busy doers sometimes find little time for during hectic days. The wise and patient Christian elder always seems to make time to lift up those God has chosen to carry on their work as well as those in need of His touch. Prayer is a much valued responsible work in and of itself. It truly is a mission. Praying out of an obedient heart for God is a sweet aroma sent up to Him and a blessing to those of the younger set and those growing older right along with us. Getting older does not have to be a time to sit idly by and wait for our home going out of boredom and loneliness. We can share God's mercy and gifts with others and care for the ones we have in our lives. Searching, while listening to others for ways to help, is always God honoring. Life can present problems that require council from someone who has been there. The older and wise adult will understand like no other and is able to share God's ways of dealing with the issue from their lifetime of experience.

So, no matter what you think you have become on the outside, God has his reasons. Time well spent serving others doesn't have to stop with old age. The Christian doesn't retire his faith and duty. Older people who have honed their heart to please God are a witness of God's faithfulness for their grandchildren learning as they go and others who wonder how *they* will do at this stage in life. God becomes our beauty and Jesus shines in our hearts to give us strength for every circumstance.

> "He has made everything beautiful in its time. He has also set eternity in the hearts of men; yet they cannot fathom what God has done from the beginning to end," Ecclesiastes 3:11.

> *"Charm is deceptive, and beauty is fleeting; but a woman who fears the Lord is to be praised," Proverbs 31:30.*

I have watched my mother, Marie, and mother-in-law, Ruth, as they aged deal with their years with grace and dignity. To both sides of the family, they have been the example of strength, faithfulness and trust in God. Ruth recently died of cancer at 84 after many years of illness. In her last year of life, she continued to drive to work and kept up with politics while mentoring others in the faith. Marie, age 94 keeps a prayer list of those in need. In a nursing facility now, nearly legally blind and dealing with diabetes she still reads her large print Bible with a magnifying glass every day, prays and talks with others about the Lord. She keeps up with friends and her relatives. Many outside the family have called her "Mom" because of her generous understanding methods. Although both had careers and raised families, Jesus took center stage. It can be done until the last breath of life. I feel honored to have had them both in my life.

THE FAVORITE BLOUSE

While sorting through her clothes, my daughter, Britt, looked at her once beloved blouse and held it up in my direction. "What" I said, "You're getting rid of that?" "Yes. You like it; you can have it, Mom." "Oh, I do love it, are you sure?" "Yes." "Thanks."

You see it's a wardrobe staple, a silky long sleeve black tee. It's as comfortable as a pajama top, yet a fashion must. Good for any occasion, it looks as nice with a pair of jeans as under a suit jacket. In summer, wear it with the sleeves pushed up, down in an air conditioned restaurant, under a sweater in winter and around the house for lounging. I'm certainly glad it has had staying power as it has been around a long time. It feels good, it's roomy, yet fitted, and never goes out of style.

Come to think of it, I'm reminded of the clothes the Israelites wore in the desert. God saw fit to give them clothes that would last 40 years while they wandered around and around trying to decide whether or not they would trust the God who had brought them through so many situations. He had rescued them, protected them and guided them. All that He asked for was obedience. That doesn't seem like much to ask for when the only true God freed them from bondage and supplied all their needs. Would He do the same for me? I would have to watch and wait.

"Mark!" You wouldn't believe what I just did." Somehow, as the words came out, I knew He would. I was painting our bedroom trim, in the favorite blouse. I didn't think I had any paint on my clothes. I threw my black blouse in the laundry when I was through working and at the end of the day, I washed it. When I brought it up out of the washer, BOOM right on the sleeve cuff there were spots of white paint! Why didn't I take that blouse off and put on a work shirt while painting in that room? I don't know, it just felt good and of course I'd be careful.

"It's ruined. I'll never be able to replace it! They don't make them like this anymore." I moaned.

"Come here." said Mark. I rushed past him and ran to the sink. In my frantic state, Mark gave instructions. He grabbed a glass of water. "Now put that sleeve down in the water and leave it there for three or four days. The water will soften that hardened paint and off it will come." I must admit I pulled it up a few times and refilled the glass several times. Where was that water going? I noticed the next day that it had traveled down the sleeve and drenched the entire blouse. Not only had it soaked the blouse, the counter was wet and the water was traveling down the counter top. I quickly cleaned the sink out and made room for the glass and blouse. The counter had to be sopped up. The water had no boundaries. It permeated everything, as a sleeve soaking in a glass of water triggered my memory of Jesus' words. "If anyone is thirsty, let him come to me and drink. "Whoever believes in me, as the Scripture has said, streams of living water will flow from within him." John 7:37-38 "There is a river whose streams make glad the city of God" spoken of in Psalms 46:4 is that ever flowing supply from God to you and me through the Word of God.

Just as my blouse drank up the water in the glass and it overflowed on to the counter top so does the spirit of God in the lives of people willing to be saturated with Him. Thinking, reading, and dwelling on God's truths can only result in a contagious overflow of joy from within.

As long as I kept filling the glass, my blouse was being worked on, the paint was softening and it would come out. Our hearts need softening. We need working on always. The water that comes from Jesus is unending, ever flowing for our benefit, for our life and growth.

He is a fountain, a bottomless well, a bubbling stream where we can become one with Him so to be imbued, filled to capacity. This is His plan and His desire, that we are filled with His spirit to the fullest extent, the greatest amount. Our worldly propensity is in the process of changing as our sin filled hearts are made clean by the washing of the Word of God.

Jump into the fountain. Lean against its rumbling vibrations so that you feel and experience His power. Stay a while. Stay always. It will wash away the care,

Love From Every Angle

the hurt, and answer your wonderings. Others will find that your rough edges are not as noticeable as time goes by, but more like a river stone in an old mill stream that is appealing and unusually smooth to the fingertips- A keeper.

One of my favorite hymns was written by a man named William Cowper after an attack of madness. When coming to his senses, He wrote:

"There is a fountain filled with blood drawn from Emmanuel's veins; and sinners plugged [plunged] beneath that flood lose all their guilty stains."

Have you a stain you've been living with that has you in turmoil? Don't make it a keeper. Lay it in the water of God's Word that washes away the stain and brings new life to you again.

Did the paint come out? Yes. It took a little longer than I expected, but the results and lessons I learned were precious. The truths He showed me are never out of style, never wear out and can't be damaged.

COME CLEAN

Studying Chapter 6 of II Corinthians I read Paul's words to his fellow Christians in the young and immature church at Corinth. He spoke to them in the most loving way, yet he was also extremely frank. When you think of the hours, days, months and years he spent teaching and training people in the faith, it was imperative that he do just that. The purpose of his ministry was clear and his vision and focus was on completion.

I know there have been people in our lives that have had similar influence on us. The people God uses in our lives may not necessarily be those we would choose, yet He knows exactly the people we need to demonstrate His love and concern for us.

I noticed the word *sincere* in this chapter and my ears perked up. I wanted to know more about its meaning. In a letter, we might start out with "Dear Sir," and end with, "Sincerely Yours". What does that mean?

I learned that the Latin derivative for sincere meant "without wax." When I read that, I immediately thought of our early days of living in Raleigh. We wanted to find the historical places and neighborhood traditions of our town for our children. One of the first places we visited was the original Manor house, Mordecai, located in the downtown area. It was a fascinating house to visit. Several generations of a single family of peoples lived there for 179 years during the years 1785-1964. You can read about their history in the book <u>Gleanings from Long Ago</u> by Ellen Mordecai. The tours were free and we set out to get a sense of Raleigh's history from this family's estate. We packed our three children in the car and drove over to the white house with the strong porch columns. The grounds were well manicured and the house gave you a feeling that sent you back many years with its old library, parlor, large rooms and a wide architectural staircase. I could imagine living there.

While our group of visitors entered the parlor the guide told us the story behind the screen set on the piano. Many colonial women would use the wax from candles to cover the scars on their faces as a result of having had pox. When playing the piano, they put a screen up in front of the candles to shield their face from the heat. They also put screens up in front of the fireplace to do the same. This was too fascinating! Many years later I learned that men, during this time period, used the wax for the same purpose of hiding their scars. It was one of the first forms of make-up. I'm sure both genders were afraid someone would find them unattractive if they saw them for their true appearance.

Love From Every Angle

There is an old line my father used in my childhood when he wanted to make me laugh, knowing I was in a pout. While I was trying to keep a straight face, he would get right up close to me and say, "Don't smile or you'll crack your face!" It worked every time. In no time at all he could make me laugh again. I wonder if that saying was passed down from this practice of using wax on one's face. Maybe that is why we see so many somber expressions in old paintings. They didn't want to "crack" a smile!

Another popular old saying was, "Mind your own bee's wax!" I have heard children use this remark in a joking way to humorously tell their peers to mind their own business. There are a couple of meanings from the 1800's. The first was a warning for ladies not to stare at another woman's waxed face and the other was meant as a warning to keep a careful distance from the heat of the fireplace, for their own good of course. I don't know which would be worse. It's not polite to stare and also, they wouldn't want to risk the chance of having a facial meltdown. It sounds primitive doesn't it?

Let's get back to Paul. He was open and forward before these people he loved with all his heart. He knew his mission was to help them to understand the entire Gospel of truth in a clean, genuine, nonpretentious way. How important that was! Obviously, these baby Christians needed someone who would be willing to speak up. Paul would be the one to bring the whole message of God to their table. The veil covering their hearts and minds came from mingling and mixing their new found faith in Jesus Christ with old worship habits of their former heathen lives.

The Corinthian church was getting extremely close to the pure truth and experiencing unadulterated love up close and personal. Paul was validating his credentials to them as a servant of Christ on a regular basis. Would they crack? That business was God's. Paul only had to do his work for the Savior.

The Latin root of sincere explains that dishonest sculptors as well as some potters in Rome and Greece would camouflage the flaws in their work with wax to deceive the viewing public. Therefore, a sculpture that did not use wax to cover flaws was considered to be an honest artisan. Paul would be a great example of a worker without wax in his motives for Christ and his love in spite of the many hardships and trials he encountered while ministering to people of all sorts. It seemed to matter more to him to be pure in his dealings with people than to be welcomed as a mere good buddy that would overlook their old sins of heathen worship practices and say it will pass the inspection of God. He knew that God expects us to come clean and face the truth about ourselves. He will take us, scars and all, and make us a new creation in Christ. "He who conceals his sin does not prosper, but whoever confesses and renounces them finds mercy", Proverbs 28:13. There is no need to cover up who we really are or to cover the truth of The Gospel. It speaks for itself. All that we need for cover is love.

ANCHORED IN LOVE

You might have told a few people, "There's a lot on my plate. I can't handle another thing!" To add to our rushed lives, unexpected tasks come up that demand attention while keeping up with our regular, grueling schedule. Why, with all these *things* are we not all thin, thin, thin? With the pace we run and the details we have to take care of in a 24 hour period, we sometimes resemble stretched rubber bands. We are bending and extending continually for what comes along. We had *better* be flexible!

Get up. Scarf down breakfast. Run out the door to work, but don't forget to put gas in the car. Phew! Call a friend. Pay the bills. Clean and shop. Be taxi driver, mentor, teacher, cook, and try to make room in the evening to relax. Responsibilities build in life and we can feel as though our day is spent in a pressure cooker. I owned one when we were first married. In fact, I still have it. I use it to cook all sorts of meals for the family. When the tiny pressure weight on top of the lid begins to rock, I know it's time to turn down the heat and let off some steam. If the lid isn't on correctly, I will be in for a nasty accident. The top of the cooker can go flying and burn a person badly. To prevent that, I have to focus my mind on what I am doing or suffer the consequences. I love that kitchen pot though because it cooks meat quickly and makes it tender and juicy.

Over the last 10 years, life has been a little intense for my family. I'll share some highlights in order to give you an idea of what I mean by *intense*. In 1998, I was diagnosed with a brain tumor and, although recovery was hard, my surgery was a success. The following year my husband was diagnosed with Lyme disease and suffered effects lasting 4 years. My mother-in-law had a brain aneurism and lung cancer twice. My sister and brother-in-law died within 2 years of each other, and my father recently died of Alzheimer's disease. We remain a family of faith and God has been good as friends have prayed for us. He has shown us His mercy and healed our wounds. We are very grateful to say the least.

Sometimes our world begins to rock and we have to let off the steam. This afternoon I was reminded of the wonderful hymn, *It is well with my Soul* by H.G Spafford. He was a man who experienced tremendous pressure and great personal loss. In the Chicago fire of 1871 he lost all of his real estate holdings. One year prior to that, his son died. Just two years after the fire Mr. Spafford wanted to help his dear friend and Christian leader D.L. Moody with a campaign in Great Britain, but business matters prevented his travel. His wife and four daughters went on ahead. He would meet up with them some days later.

On November 22, 1873 there was an awful ship collision involving the S.S. Ville Du Havre, the ship his family was on, and the English ship Lochearn. Several days after the survivors reached Cardiff, Wales Mr. Spafford received a cable from his wife reading, "Saved alone." His four daughters were gone. Now that is not only pressure, but overwhelming grief and pain.

Despite his pain, he was able to write this inspirational hymn as he traveled to his grieving wife. He was aware that God's love strengthens and anchors us no matter our life's circumstance. He didn't just create that belief. It developed from an ongoing abiding with God. He knew God's nature, His power, and His faithfulness that sees us through pressure and heartache, mountaintops and valleys.

I had just been hurrying around to ready the house for my mother-in- law. She would be returning to our home from the hospital following surgery. The phone rang and I had to take care of other business. The countertop we were having installed in our kitchen had a few problems as did the new cabinets. I looked around at our tools and mess of construction and started to sing. No one was home but me as I sang out the words to, *It is well with my Soul*; two or three lines was all it took. "Whatever my lot thou has taught me to say, 'It is well, it is well, with my soul'."

Describing the sorrow that came in waves as the sea billows that rolled in and swept his daughters away, H.G. Spafford was still able to be at peace within. I find it interesting to note that he wrote,

"Thou hast *taught* me to say, 'It is well, it is well with my soul.'" That comes from lessons learned while spending time with his Savior. I breathed in deeply, and ran upstairs to iron.

This is not to say that I have not cried and felt the weight of life's issues. However, I am assured that God will take care of me in spite of the things I encounter and not give me more than I can handle. God is the underpinning for life's situations. When leaning on His arms I don't have to worry that He will give way and let me fall. I may lose my balance, but He is there to steady my steps. What a comfort. God is building a person of strength each time we obey and acknowledge Him. His power runs through us to handle the circumstances of life. He guides and plans for this building to take place and gives us everything we need as a believer to finish the work. That understanding brings amazing peace of heart.

> *"Oh peace that overshadows life*
> *Stay with me throughout storm and strife*
> *Give me the understanding needed to see*
> *It's not me that brackets strong my way, but Thee."*

SAVIOR ALONE

There has been quite a bit of talk recently in the news about an influential politician selling out his party for political gain. Jockeying for higher office has his party up in arms and on the other side of the aisle they are thrilled with his direction that they believe will serve them well. What lengths will we go to when positioning ones self for fame or power?

Our human inclination has us first seeking our own wishes before considering God's plan. History tells of the trials of getting to the top in politics, business or other human endeavors. It is not always a success story. There are people apt to be hurt and suffer as some strive to be seated at the table of honor. God has a different plan for us. He wants the best for us and has called us to be thoughtful of others, no matter what our estate in life.

Of course, not being in the political arena I only know the story from watching the news and what I read. As I reflected on the facts that I did know, God began to instruct me about His sovereign dealings in our affairs. God helped me understand the relationship with life's happenings and heart attitudes. Sometimes while driving in the middle of traffic God reminds me how His hand controls the events of our time. What a stress reliever it is to understand that Jesus leads and teaches in many different ways as we move about within our daily lives year after year.

I don't need to be at the top of the heap in this world, like a powerful politician, to know I can enter His presence. At any time He will be glad to give me audience, hear me and teach me His ways. He enters whatever I am doing and helps me make right choices. Whether it is a political decision, work atmosphere or home life, God is interested and willing to help me think clearly. He works things out in my mind and heart using the examples written down in His Word. That's what having a friend in Jesus is all about. He gently guides and supports. I would not be so arrogant to assume I always choose correctly, but God continues to work with me.

Have you ever had a friend who thinks they know you better than you know yourself? Jesus is the only one who knows us perfectly. I am so happy that God knows the rest of the story of my life. He alone knows how it will all turn out. That is also true of the things beyond our control.

There is always speculation for future events in the political arena. It is the job of some in the media to not only report on the latest stories, but also give us food for thought. What will happen if this one or that one wins the presidency? Will we go down a wrong path and take our country in a direction that does not bring honor to God? Will we remain the strongest country in the world?

When we are uncertain about changing headlines and the frenzy of debates and who is in charge, God tells us He has been and always will be in charge of events. When we concentrate on our purpose for living and God's ability to manage, calm will take over our concerned mind.

Remember Jesus' countless trials with His disciples when they questioned His identity and purpose? They didn't get it right from the start. It took a long time of watching and listening to Jesus and just being with Him. Nevertheless, in His timing, He opened their minds to understand and see who He was and what to do for Him and others in their time period no matter who was running things.

Have you ever asked Him to open your understanding so that you would better know the meaning of the Scriptures or why He has you where you are right now in your life? He will deepen your understanding as you ask Him questions and speak with Him regularly. If you know nothing more to say than "Help Lord" He will hear you and meet you right where you are. He understands the intricacies of our thoughts and heart longings. His hand is ready to take yours. Open the Scriptures and get the real history of mankind, the personalities, the victories and the failures. Look at what God's response is when we trust Him for the current and future events of our nation and others. It is the Savior alone who is dependable through the years no matter which political party holds the reins of power. 11 Chronicles 15:2b says

"The Lord is with you when you are with him. If you seek him he will be found by you, but if you forsake him he will forsake you." I don't want to be without Him in the situations of life. I am so thankful that He comes along side those who want Him to be with them. Psalms 40:1 says "I waited patiently for the Lord; he turned to me and heard my cry. He lifted me out of the slimy pit, out of the mud and mire; he set my feet on a rock and gave me a firm place to stand." The mud and mire reminds me of the deceitful tactics of politicians and others that has become the norm these recent years. It is hard to rely on anything or anyone.

Sometimes the security we count on here proves to be no more than shifting sand beneath changing tides. We look up from the paper or T.V. news one day only to realize that we have drifted off course from what our founding fathers intended. We never would imagine that life would take us far away from basic truths that give us a strong foundation to work from. We don't have a crystal ball that tells us the future and that all will be easy. Those answers are in God's hands. We must merely be tied to what is true and be in ready mode to deal with things based on trust in God. Politicians come and go, wars and illness come our way and we have to be able to face them without crumbling. We must trust Jesus with our hearts, not a talk show host or political guru as powerful and influential as they may be. Their opinions constantly change.

It is the responsibility of believers to pray for our nation and to lift our leaders up to Him on a daily basis. 11 Corinthians 7:14 says "If my people, who are called by my name, will humble themselves and pray and seek my face and turn from their wicked ways, then I will hear from heaven and will forgive their sin and will heal their land."

With those instructions to believers who choose to walk the path of humility and purpose, open the paper, and watch the news. Discuss topics at hand and take them to Jesus in prayer. Measure all matters against Scripture. Use the power to reason that the Lord has given you and let Him guide your heart and mind.

A DOG'S DAY OUT

Often when I head down one of the main streets near my home I pass an apartment complex and witness a man's struggle with his dog. Decked out in what looks to be a rhinestone collar glistening in the sun, this well dressed dog's jewels are then followed by a leash with a man attached at the end. This man must think his dog is something special to dress him in such splendor. There are many walkers around lunch time. However, while this man wants to take his pup out for a stroll, the dog clearly has another idea.

Standing still with arms folded yet continuing to hold the leash, the expression on this man's face is priceless. Hound dog is taking a sun bath! "It's just too hot out, Dad," he seems to be communicating to his master, "I can't get up—haven't got the strength. If you'll wait just a minute, I'll be with you and we'll do that walk we talked about." The master waits.

Now one thing I am assuming is that this man would not want to carry this heavy, low-to-the-ground breed of animal around—to his dog's chagrin. This man is dressed in suit pants and a white shirt; not appropriate attire for such animal luxuries. What's an owner to do? If I get there at just the right moment I can see the master of this stretched out pooch making attempts to lead him on, but the pup will not budge. The man moves to the right and then left and *still* they make no progress. This dog is of his own inclination and the man's arms fold again. I chuckle as I drive by.

This man is probably just home on his lunch hour. He wants to take his dog outside at midday so he won't have any surprises awaiting him when he gets home at night. Once in a while the dog lifts his eyes to peek at the man on the end of the leash, but there is no desire to get up or willingness to strain himself for this waiting master. I am frustrated for this man. I never seem to come back soon enough to get the rest of the story, but I can imagine there is much of the same…standing and waiting, lying and resting.

There are some of us with similar response mannerisms. Our Master and God, places *sonship* around our heart and leads us when we belong to Him. Rather than a collar of ownership, the believer now has a *heart covenant* with his God declaring the agreement between them. This person has admitted their need to be reconciled to God and He washes him clean and fills his mind and heart with His spirit.

When one commits to obey the Father and Master, there is mutual love between them. It is up to this person to follow God's lead and let the Father direct him to the areas He wishes the believer to explore. His lead never leaves your heart, for His commitment to His children is sure. Our hearts sometime becomes lazy to His will and our eyes and ears are not in tune to the Master's voice. We can sometimes lay unyielding and feel neither the gentle tug nor the direction of His bidding. Has His hand beckoned you to "come"? Would you rather lie down and close your eyes to opportunities He has for you?

My mother used to tell me as a girl, "pray for the desire" to do whatever I was struggling with in the Lord's service. That was excellent advice. Perhaps, we humans need a refresher course that will once again renew our devotion to our Master and Lord. We, like the pup, can be in the habit of stretching out for a nap and resting—rather than doing. It's difficult to change on our own. Our Master waits. Time passes and soon the outing is over.

We have time here on earth to be a faithful follower of Christ and walk closely by His side. Every day we are given 24 hours. We have hours to sleep, to work, to listen and obey whatever it is He wants us to do in the community, our home, our study and with people of all sorts. If we say, "No, I don't feel like it", we lose out and our opportunity ends.

When watching a dog dutifully and cheerfully obey his master, it is a joy. All are amazed with this partnership they both enjoy. Wouldn't it be a pleasure for the man in the above scenario to open the door to his *best friend* and get a welcome he would be pleased to get, obedience and affection? "Oh I'm so glad to see you!" the dog would show as he came bounding over to his master. "And I am so glad to come home for a bit to spend moments with you, dear friend," the master would in turn express.

Is it a joy to be with your Master? Have you made Him proud and glad with your attention to Him and His requests? Maybe you have merely peeked at the opportunities He gives you. Have you kept Him waiting and told Him, "Next time—I'll be right with you. Just give me a moment, and I will do that thing it was you asked of me."

I don't think He is pleased with that response, do you? We have this moment right now to tell Him otherwise. Won't you show Him that He is important to you and you are more than happy to comply with His wishes? The strain you probably feel in the relationship would disappear. Once again, thank Him for that *sonship* He gave deep in your heart that proves you are worth everything to Him as He calls you His own. That s*onship* should shine out of you like an expensive necklace in the light of the Son so that even passersby would take notice as they say, "Now there is a different person. He has purpose and joy. What is it that makes him special?"

We want to be willing to say along with David in Psalm 143:10, "Teach me to do your will, for you are my God; may your good Spirit lead me on level ground." Oh Friend, allow God to search your heart to see if there is anything that hinders you from unreservedly following His lead.

TALL CANDLES

While cleaning out my attic, I came across a gift from my husband's dear aunt. It is a beautiful poem she found in an old book. It was written by Gertrude Hanson. Jessie framed it with a soft green mat and placed a lovely flower at the bottom right side of the frame. We have had this for years and as we change things around in the house, our gift was put away temporarily for a later time. Coming across it again, I stopped what I was doing to read the melodic words once again. Aunt Jessie was a sensitive woman who had a heart of gold and a love of words. The poem reads:

God, light tall candles in my heart,
Make every dim-lit space
So glowing that no evil thing
Can find a hiding space

God light tall candles in my heart,
Lest I should fail to see
That Thy word is the cup of strength
For all humanity,

Burn brightly candles in my heart…
No soul has ever trod
Earth's twisted ways of faith without
Deep inner light from God.

Gertrude Hanson

It was not out of character that she gave us this poem. It was a thoughtful gesture on her part. As a gleaner she was always sharing poems, thoughts, and articles she had read. She might at any time step out of her car, with her writings in hand, and begin to read to us what she had penned while watching a bird on a ledge. Her writings were always God related. She saw Him everywhere.

Mark has always told me that there was never anything out of bounds when talking with this fine human being. She was one of the most accepting people he has ever known and he loved her very much. She never made anyone feel small or foolish. She was very gracious that way and it was especially meaningful to children. They absorb maybe more than we adults do. Belief in your motives and words are taken to heart and remembered sometimes forever when we are young. Mark and she would talk for hours on end during visits to his sweet aunt's home.

Aunt Jessie was a gifted person to say the least, and it showed in her love of crafts, books and talent for cooking. She was a gourmet cook and even had a column in the paper showcasing her recipes from around the world. Her specialty was Asian Cuisine and she would invite the lonely, the neighbors as well as my husband and his friends for delicious lunches when they were working in Melbourne, Florida. Aunt Jessie taught my husband, Mark, the art of flower making when he was around ten years old. This was before mass production of artificial flowers. They made enough flowers together to fill a large birdcage. It was big enough to fit 6 grown men inside it. It would be hung in a hotel lobby. They also made flower arrangements for other rooms in public places. Each petal and leaf had to be made by hand, and baked in her kitchen oven. One had to be a patient person to do this tedious work, let alone teach a child the skill. The time was well spent, as today Mark can craft just about anything, likes to cook, and certainly enjoys stimulating conversation.

My husband not only loved his aunt, but valued her priorities. People were very important to her. A tidy house hers was not, but love was preeminent there.

Her life had a hard beginning. Born to a teenage girl whose marriage had gone terribly wrong, Jessie's mother was forced into divorce and the children were doled out to family and friends. Little Jessie was given to neighbors her mother barely knew. She was not raised with nor saw her brother and sister for many years. Richard and Ruth were living with their grandmother when one day they were snatched away to live elsewhere. Their mother became afraid and superstitious.

Although one might wonder whether this could have a happy ending, you can be assured that God had a plan for each of their lives. God found His way into their world and the three children, Jessie, Ruth and Richard each had someone tell them about the saving life of Christ that changed their life's direction.

Jessie's life was about to change drastically. When she was an adult she gave her life to the Savior, Jesus Christ and became a missionary to Australia along with her husband, Merle. They went there to help build a church and together taught the natives as well as had meals with them. While there, Jessie ate some tainted meat. Unaware, she did not realize the danger she was in.

Twenty years later living in the United States, and in a ministry for missionaries home on furlough, she began to act strangely. After attempting to figure out what was wrong, they discovered that her symptoms were similar to Alzheimer's disease. She was very ill. Jesse died of what is commonly known as Mad Cow Disease.

Hers was a life lived simply to glorify the Lord Jesus. Whenever I look at that sweet poem, and remember Aunt Jessie, I know we were in the presence of Tall Candles. The light of her life shone brightly.

Have you ever met a person like my husband's aunt? Have they been a positive spiritual influence and inspiration in your life? Would that we too ask the Lord to light tall candles in our hearts so that what others see would be the inner light of God. For it is not what we are handed in life, but what we hand Him. "Let your light shine before men, that they may see your good deeds and praise your Father in heaven." Mathew 5:16.

SMOOTHING ROUGH EDGES

Did you ever think your parents were telling you the truth when they said "Work hard and long and it will really pay off in the end?" Most of us could not see the long term benefits or the importance in it. Even today's man or woman believes they can achieve the ultimate in an abbreviated amount of time. Everyone is on the fast track these days and has grown accustomed to the speed with which we fly through life. We hurry to work, hurry to get to the dry cleaners before it closes, and rush to the bus, the train, and airport. Our children for the most part hurry to get the chores done and their homework finished. We even hurry through our meals to move onto the next thing we need to do. Everyone wants a shortcut to meal preparation. I was appalled when my grown children suggested heavy duty paper plates one holiday, but for this particular season it did make things faster for clean-up and there were so many of us wanting to play games and run around after we ate.

This last spring our in-town grandson, Haddon, wanted me to buy him a rock tumbler. We couldn't find it for the longest time and thought it was probably not available anymore. On our way out the door he spotted it high on a store shelf. It promised the manufacture of fine jewelry making for *Mom*, stone key chains, shiny treasures and grinding. "Oh, the grinding!" Well, with so many possibilities, we brought it down from the shelf and had a good look. "We can use it to grind rocks from the lake near by!" he tried to convince me. You see, collecting rocks for this young boy was right up there with pirate treasure hunting. We brought it back to our house and set it up. It came with rocks, and different materials for different steps and a grinder. I read the instructions with his Appa and we set it up and plugged it in. You see, this small version of what takes years, was to teach a child the wonder in the process that brings about beauty and smoothness in a rock. Although this sounded like a great idea to Haddon, it sounded so loud and annoying to us we could barely think. One might have thought we had a cement mixer in the kitchen churning 24-7. That was the point wasn't it? Turn and grind and never stop until the job was completed. We finally unplugged it and put it on the back deck where the French doors would muffle the sound of the constant grind. We kept it going for a couple of weeks until Haddon asked to take a peek at the progress we were making. When we saw no change to the rocks at all we realized that we forgot to put in the right solution to speed up the process. We too, must have been in too great a hurry to read the steps and get it right. So, we returned to the directions.

"Okay, what's the problem?" We got the box down and took another look. Inside the box along with the directions was a small bag with the sand compound necessary to get the job done. All that noise had been making a pitiful effort. This small package made all the difference in the world. We had an opportunity to see the fruits of correct application.

We all do a lot of spinning and grinding, but unless we have the right solution we are not going to achieve the desired effect for our lives. I recently told someone who asked how my husband and I were doing, that we were very busy and running around trying to get it all done like a chicken with its head cut off. Our days are full and schedules are packed aren't they?

Paul, the wonderful apostle spoke to the Corinthian Christians about doing things in an orderly fashion. He wanted them to read the directions, listen if you will, and get their doctrine straight. They wanted to be Christians and yet they did not believe in Christ's resurrection from the dead. In 1 Corinthians 15:1 he spelled it out for them. "I want to remind you of the gospel I preached to you, which you received and on which you have taken your stand." Chapter 15:3 says "For what I received I passed on to you as of first importance: That Christ died for our sins according to the Scriptures, that he was buried, that he was raised on the third day according to the Scriptures."

On further in I Corinthians he let them know if Christ did not die then he was just another good man that lived an exceptional life and died. End of story.

God sent His son, Jesus, to die for us while here on earth because we needed to be redeemed from our sins by the only perfect lamb, once and for all time. Jesus was completely and utterly different and separate from all men. While here on earth He was fully God and fully man at the same time. There would be no more need for ritual animal sacrifice. That, although necessary, prepared us for the one who would come to sacrifice His sinless self one time for all of mankind. He was the first to rise from the dead and never die again. God raised Christ from the dead so that we who believe might also be raised to newness of life here and now. Before we are a believer and have accepted Christ as our Savior, we are dead in our sins. At the moment of our belief, our life truly begins. After we die a physical death, believers live with Him forever. We have life everlasting after our work for God on earth is finished. There is hope. There is reason to look forward to every day as an opportunity of blessing and growth.

Let's begin putting first things first. The resurrection of Christ is essential to a changed life. We needed that essential bag of solution in Haddon's rock tumbler to finish the work of the grinder; to bring the process to the full affect. "If Christ has not been raised, your faith is futile; you are still in your sins." (Corinthians 15:17) Just as the rocks did not change we are not changed. Life is just as useless as an empty rotating grinder. We go through the motions. We are in what is known as the daily grind.

Correct doctrine is vital to our lives. We either believe all of what Christ did for us or we are lost and confused about what ingredients are needed for things to work together between God and man. We don't need to live an empty life. It can be fulfilling as God shows us his wonders and we follow His instructions yielding to His ways.

TENDER HEART

If one were to ask me about my grandchildren, Lyndsey, Luke and Haddon they would hear many wonderful stories I keep in my memory bank. Our son, Derek and his wife, Amy just had a new baby girl, Brooke. What joy! Our latest thrill was hearing on Father's Day that our youngest daughter, Britt and her husband Neil are expecting their first child this winter. This is a group of extraordinary kids! I imagine you feel the same way about your children or grandchildren. Children are often so cheerful and fun. They are always discovering new facts and exploring ways to make life more interesting. Observing children gives us insight into what God might have meant when He said to come to Him as a child.

Children believe, trust and depend. As they grow older they often lose their sense of dependence. When they are young they have the kind of faith that, where God is concerned, is both simple and profound. It is the kind of faith that God wants us to have and maintain. He would not want us to become so self reliant that we leave Him out of our lives or think of Him only when it is to our benefit.

Often we adults think we can handle our own affairs without spiritual guidance as we forget that we need to be as dependant as a child. We learn as we grow older to allow our priorities and possessions to set our agenda. Many have even become leery of the Christian faith walk, asking "What will it require of me? Will it mean I must give up the lifestyle I enjoy?" Sometimes as adults the heart becomes calloused and hard toward things above. We don't want anything to come between us and our comfortable world.

What a contrast to the heart of a child, so trusting and tender. Children put their hands out and surrender all of themselves for friendship and love. In their innocence, they have nothing to lose. They are new to relationships. Fear of putting their all into one isn't there. They love and respond to love without reservation. They hear of God's love and believe, wanting it for themselves and others.

A sweet memory of my childhood days was a session with my dog while alone in the kitchen. I told him of the love of the Lord Jesus. My arm tightly hugged him as I genuinely was practicing on him what I would later come to know in reality. I remember saying "Did you know that God made you? He loves you!" I had heard the story so many times through my parents. The dogs we raised were a part of our family. As a child I wanted to share the truth with them as well as others. Who better to tell what I was learning to be true?

When does that childlike zeal for God leave our hearts? When do we become indifferent? Perhaps as adults we have become too attached to "our stuff" and our interest in spiritual affairs fades. There are many more things that hold our attention. We desire to be entertained with the latest gadget that we find amusing. Somehow we seem to think we deserve the best, so we need more to keep us satisfied and secure. We have become too materially full and the hunger is just not there anymore for the things of God. We are lulled into believing they hold the measuring stick of our worth in this life. Pride before others and keeping up with the neighbors replaces the once tender heart toward God. We will do whatever it takes to make the grade in this life. Unfortunately this is a vacant promise that can never really satisfy.

Are you tired of striving for more things, but never feeling satisfied? Are you tired of feeling empty? Then ask God to give you back that tender heart, a heart that believes, trusts, and depends. Ask Him to give you a heart of thankfulness for a sacrifice given up for us in Christ Jesus. He sought no comfort for Himself, but desired to bring us back into fellowship with Him through great suffering.

In Luke 23:39 it says that a criminal who hung on a cross beside Jesus hurled insults at Him: "Aren't you the Christ? Save yourself and us!" Although this criminal had an awareness of Christ he was unbreakable and cynical to the end.

There were two criminals crucified beside Christ that day. We don't know their background stories or what caused them to commit crimes that led to crucifixion. "But the other criminal rebuked the first, 'Don't you fear God,' he said, 'since we are under the same sentence? We are punished justly, for we are getting what our deeds deserve. But this man has done nothing wrong.' Then he said 'Jesus, remember me when you come into your kingdom.'" (Luke 23:40-42).

Oh that we would understand! Jesus warns, "What good is it for a man to gain the whole world, yet forfeit his soul?" (Mark 8:36) Each of us deserves the death penalty for breaking God's laws.

The thief on the cross was once a child, sweet and tender. Somehow within God's miraculous mystery this thief's tender heart was given back to him. Children know almost instinctively when adults are genuine. They can tell when adults are faking it as well as when they are sincere about their love for them. He knew Jesus was real! Hanging on the cross he finally recognized Jesus as God's son, and then saw himself for the wretched man he had become. The invisible ties that had kept him restrained and in sin were loosened, allowing him to experience the pulse of a God-centered healthy heart in the midst of his dying. He became alive to Christ in his last hours. Because he confessed, he was saved to wake up in paradise forever with the Savior. God can do the same for any person!

Can you imagine the pliability that came to this man's heart through this recognition of the Savior and His purity? Coupled with admission of his own sin, the exchange that took place between this criminal and the Son of God instantly changed his eternal destiny. He acknowledged Jesus personally and Jesus spoke love to him when He answered, "I tell you the truth, today you will be with me in Paradise." (Luke 23:43).

Jesus gave the man the gift of eternal life in spite of the fact that He, who was without sin, was being humiliated and tortured. Can you imagine the effort it took for them to even speak while on their crosses? Yet history was made and reconciliation was taking place between God and man.

Reconciliation happens every day, even now, for the person who will place their faith and trust in Christ. In Corinthians 13:13, Paul says, "Now these three remain: faith, hope, and love. But the greatest of these is love." We know why children are loved. They are adorable! But, sometimes we adults are not so lovable. The Bible tells us in John 3:16 that "God so loved the world that he gave his one and only son that whosoever believes in him shall not perish but have eternal life." That means He cared enough to sacrificially die for children, teenagers, adults and the aged.

When I was a preteen, God allowed me to take part in helping a desperate, lonely, mentally ill woman. She had been committed to an institution and was home for what she was told would be her last visit. I was at her house playing with her children, when I heard sobs coming from her bedroom. When entering her room after being called, all she could get out was "Wendy, get your mother, get your mother!" I bolted out the door and jumped the stone wall separating our yards, and ran to our house. My mother, being a proactive Christian woman, grabbed her Bible and came with me. Mom had met with her before, but this day this poor in spirit woman finally understood that Jesus loved her. I heard her say "You mean, Marie, that Jesus loves ME? How simple yet profound. Jesus loves me.

With childlike awe her outlook and heart took a u-turn and she accepted God's message of love to individuals. Yes, we as adults can experience hope, assurance and eternal life when we trust Christ as a child with tenderness of heart. May we each ask God to activate faith, hope and love within us and rejuvenate our indifferent heart.

How Deep the Father's Love for Us
Lyrics by Stuart Townend

How deep the Father's love for us,
How vast beyond all measure
That He should give His only Son
To make a wretch His treasure.

How great the pain of searing loss,
The Father turns His face away
As wounds which mar the chosen One,
Bring many sons to glory

Behold the Man upon a cross,
My sin upon His shoulders
Ashamed I hear my mocking voice,
Call out among the scoffers

It was my sin that held Him there
Until it was accomplished
His dying breath has brought me life
I know that it is finished

I will not boast in anything
no gifts, no power, no wisdom
But I will boast in Jesus Christ
His death and resurrection

Why should I gain from His reward?
I cannot give an answer
But this I know with all my heart
His wounds have paid my ransom

Used with Permission

Can you sing that song? Does it express the experience you have had in Jesus? Are you a wretch for whom Jesus paid the price to make His own? If it does describe you then you have had that child-like faith that yields the totality of yourself to His sacrifice.

If you are not a recipient of this great love then now is the time for you to lose yourself in His love. Like the thief on the cross you can return to that which you have lost, a life of selflessness. You come to Him as a child. No preconditions. No inhibitions. He will accept you and make you His child.

FINAL THOUGHTS

Many people say that visuals nail a truth down like nothing else. I heard this poem quoted from the pulpit by a wonderful pastor that I deeply admired for years, Dr. Adrian Rogers. It impressed me so then, that it has stayed with me. While I was listening to its words I was able to picture Jesus as the active God in a person's life. I remember thinking to myself "This is so good. I want to believe God is all of these things." I wrote it down as I heard it and read it over and over. It was something that put the truth about God in simple prose. Today, through life in Christ, I have come to know that my Maker is all of these things in the fullness of reality. Life's experiences and undeniable faith in God's Word have taught me that I can trust God to be with me throughout life's journey. He is the eternal God.

As you read it I believe it will encourage you too. I want you to know that Jesus is the essence of pure and undefiled love. He is as ancient as before time and contemporary as the year in which we live. He is still at work today.

Who is Jesus?

He is
The Shield from every dart;
Balm for every smart;
The Bearer of every load;
The Companion on the road

The Door into the fold;
The Anchor that will hold!
The Shepherd of the sheep;
The Guardian of my sleep

The Friend with whom I talk;
The Way in which I walk;
The Light to show the way;
The Strength for every day

The Source of my delight;
The Song to cheer the night;
The Thought that fills my mind;
The Best of all to find-is Jesus

Author Unknown

Printed in the United States
212811BV00001B/2/P